COAL TOWN *KIDS*

Duane Radford (R) and his brother Jim (L) with their grandfather
Albert Sapeta in Coleman circa 1950

DUANE S. RADFORD

FriesenPress

One Printers Way
Altona, MB R0G 0B0
Canada

www.friesenpress.com

Copyright © 2022 by Duane S. Radford
First Edition — 2022

All rights reserved.

Book Design and Layout by: FriesenPress
Edited by: FriesenPress
Photography by Duane S. Radford unless otherwise noted.

The spelling of people's names was doubled-checked with print publications, school records, online sources, obituaries, and personal contact with Pass residents and former residents. Every effort has been made to provide the correct spelling of the names of all the people cited in this book. Any errors are the fault of the author for which he sincerely apologizes.
There are many discrepancies in place names and their origin for this part of Canada. While there are different spellings of "Crowsnest Pass" and "Crow's Nest Pass" the former spelling will (generally) be used in this book, although the mountain pass itself is correctly called the Crow's Nest Pass. No definite conclusion can be made from historical records regarding the origin of the name Crow's Nest Pass and mountain according to *A History of the Crow's Nest Pass* by William James Cousins.

ISBN
978-1-03-914486-6 (Hardcover)
978-1-03-914485-9 (Paperback)
978-1-03-914487-3 (eBook)

1. HISTORY, CANADA, PROVINCIAL, TERRITORIAL & LOCAL, PRARIE PROVINCES (AB, MB, SK)

Distributed to the trade by The Ingram Book Company

COAL TOWN KIDS

TESTIMONIAL

Alberta's Crowsnest Pass is a place of sweeping history, stunning landscapes and compelling intrigues. Duane Radford has written a very personal rendition of the post-World War II era of the Crowsnest Pass, using the stories of his family and their neighbors. It speaks to and is a reminder that our future is not divisible from our past and personal histories form important milestones to reflect on. The stories in "Coal Town Kids" are poignant, entertaining and shine a light on a time before much of what we now consider essentials would not have been normal fare. This era was one of tough, hard, poor times. Yet, despite the challenges these are stories of a time well lived by children who knew no different. Crowsnest Pass communities may have lacked wealth and amenities yet, for a kid growing up, were vibrant places filled with opportunities and experiences. Duane's book also provides insights into the impacts of past coal mining and perspectives on how that land use may still grip the Pass psyche. This book is a slice of pure, authentic Canadiana.

Lorne Fitch,
author and professional biologist

NOTE FROM THE AUTHOR

This is a non-fiction novel about the life experiences of a boy, his family, and his friends growing up in Bellevue when it was an active coal-mining town in the Crowsnest Pass, in small-town Alberta. The name Bellevue comes from the French expression "Quelle un belle vue," which means beautiful view, testament to the picture-postcard, spectacular view to the west of town.

The book also describes key historical events that shaped the character of the area. The setting of this book is on the edge of the Canadian Rockies in southwestern Alberta after World War II until the author's family moved to Calgary, Alberta, in 1963. Locals call this area "the Pass," which includes settlements along Highway 3, such as Bellevue, Hillcrest, Frank, Blairmore, and Coleman in Alberta, plus Sparwood and Fernie in British Columbia.

In the words of William James Cousins in his book *A History of the Crow's Nest Pass*, prior to 1952: "A mining area, the Crow's Nest Pass has a cosmopolitan population and has achieved a reputation as a rough, tough area with considerable drinking and brawling." Cousins's book was a dissertation for the University of Alberta that was published as a book in 1952. *Coal Town Kids* represents the first substantive non-fiction account dealing with the Pass since 1952. At the time, the Pass was a hard place for people to make a living and most people faced a lot of adversity. This book explores many of the roots of Canadian experiences during this historical period.

The book represents a first-hand account of what it was like as a kid growing up in the Pass following World War II. Some of the author's childhood friends kindly provided stories about their personal experiences. While the author never thought of his family as being poor, by today's standards, they were, as were many of his friends and neighbours.

CONTENTS

DEDICATION

This book is a tribute to my parents and grandparents, whose fortitude, hard work, and sacrifices made for a better life for me.

While this book is obviously a personal account, several friends have provided supplemental stories, their family history similar to mine. I can only imagine the hardships my grandparents faced immigrating to Canada and the challenges and danger that both of my grandfathers experienced in the coal mines, as well as my father, who also spent time in the West Canadian Collieries Ltd. Bellevue Mine. I know full well the sacrifices my parents made for me to get ahead in life. I remember how difficult life was for them at times and the heartbreak they experienced when my father's small trucking business went bankrupt.

Life for my father wasn't easy, yet he served his country in the Royal Canadian Navy during World War II, he was a founding member of the Bellevue volunteer fire department and served as an officer of Masonic Lodge of Canada. He risked his life hauling coal from mines during the winter on treacherous roads, such as the one to the Adanac Mine. My mother worked tirelessly as a housewife while we lived in the Pass and returned to the Canadian work force as a stenographer in what was then called Revenue Canada when we moved to Calgary, not retiring until she was seventy years old.

I'd also like to dedicate this book to my friends from the Pass who enriched my life; they deserve my heartfelt thanks in so many ways. As a member of the vanguard of Canada's baby boomers, I can attest that there was no established trail to follow, so we made our own.

FOREWORD

I'm deeply impressed by Mr. Radford's proven ability to expose, via writing and colourful imagery, the life and vitality—as well as the trials and tribulations—of post-World War II existence in the storied headwaters of Alberta's Crowsnest River.

It's here, in the shadow of the devastating Frank Slide (North America's deadliest rockslide), on land rocked by the 1914 Hillcrest Explosion (Canada's worst mine disaster), that Mr. Radford opens the door to adventure and discovery. He does this armed with decades of experience and an eye focused on the wealth of cultural and natural history that has surrounded him as he climbed mountains to gain a visionary perspective of the land and its people.

Mr. Radford was born in a community defined by the darkness of tragedy and untimely death. He wears these scars and carries haunting memories. He knows well how he and his generation were shaped by the often-brutal realities of life-and-death struggles to survive while fighting to forge a pathway to a better future. He's lived a life grounded in hardship, a life that's also been illuminated by the magic and beauty of shining mountains and a legacy of historical intrigue.

I believe Mr. Radford's lifelong love affair with the land of his youth, his ongoing research, and his ability to capture and convey colourful lore enables him to produce an important and valuable supplement to Canada's captivating history.

I welcome Mr. Radford's envisioned publication containing history-rich additions to this country's capture of its strong and defining roots.

David McIntyre,
forest scientist and past director of the Frank Slide Interpretive Centre

Burmis Tree Poem by Monica Field

I have felt the winds of winter tear through branches lithe and green
When I was a tiny seedling growing slowly and unseen
There before the Europeans built their homes and claimed the land
Unaware that forces of nature can't be tamed by human hand

Through the years I watched the coal mines take a fortune from
    the ground
Watched the people raise their families in the freedom they had found
Saw the slide destroy the valley, now the edges lined with trees
Prove again that life endures, though death has stacked and cut
    the sheaves

I have seen the mountains blow
And kill those working down below
I have seen the river rise
And water deluge from the skies

Now the wind blows strong as ever though the mines have come
    and gone
Bare and start, but bravely standing
I am bound to linger on

*The Burmis Tree, perhaps the most photographed tree in Canada,
beside Highway 3 near Burmis, Alberta, the eastern edge of the Crowsnest Pass.*

1

COMMUNITY

GEOGRAPHY AND HISTORY OF THE PASS

Although I spent my childhood in Bellevue, I tell most people that I grew up in "the Pass." I always felt that I was raised in a broader community than just Bellevue. Virtually all locals shorten the name of the Crowsnest Pass to the Pass.

The Crowsnest Pass is a geographic area defined by a legendary mountain pass that straddles the border between Alberta and British Columbia, extending roughly from Burmis, Alberta, to Fernie, British Columbia. The Pass has always been defined by coal and mineral mining.

Most locals would say that the unique Burmis Tree marks the start of the Pass on the Alberta side of the border. This ancient limber pine beside Highway 3 near Burmis fell on October 8, 1998, and was subsequently restored by local authorities and the Government of Alberta as a signature landmark. It is a waypoint for travellers heading to the Pass, signalling that they are almost home.

The following is an excerpt from the September 23, 2015, issue of *Shootin' the Breeze,* a Pincher Creek e-magazine, courtesy of David McIntyre, forest scientist and former director of the Frank Slide Interpretive Centre:

> *It was a treat to read Bob Pisko's—"I took that picture"—follow-up [Sept. 16, 2015 issue] to the Breeze's recent coverage*

of an "old" (circa '72) picture of the Burmis Tree, an ancient, wind-tortured limber pine widely believed to be Canada's most photographed tree.

Breeze readers may be interested to know, too, that the Gov. of Alberta issued poster pictures of the Burmis Tree that were likely taken back in the early to mid '70s, a time when the tree, and a neighboring "sister" tree, were still living. The noted poster was, as I recall, one among a series featuring celebrated Alberta heritage attractions.

What caused the Burmis Tree's death? Anecdotal reports reveal that a local high school class adopted the tree in the late '70s and, as a project, placed rocks around it and—let the drum rolls begin—fertilized the old pine. This, if not done with extreme care, would have killed the tree.

Regardless of what killed the picturesque old pine, it, lifeless and leafless since the late '70s, fell to the ground in '98. Later that same year the tree again made headlines when it, while still quite dead, rose from its deathbed to reclaim its stand as a Highway 3 sentinel. (The tree didn't, I should report, rise up without significant assistance.)

Conflicting news reports addressing the tree's age (reported to be between 200 and 700) at the time of its resurrection intrigued me, and prompted me to contact Harold Ganske, a retired forest worker and the individual said to have cored the tree to document its age.

Harold, as I recall from my conversation with him (circa '98), told me the cored tree had heart-rot, a condition typical of old trees, and that he could not, as a result, determine the tree's precise age. This noted, he, based on the extrapolation of data produced by the tree's available growth rings, was of the opinion that the tree was approximately 700 years old at the time of its death. (This, based on my own experience in coring old limber pines in this area, is a reasonable and likely age for the tree.)

The Burmis Tree, shaped by the winds of time, has many stories to tell. We know it today for its stark, skeletal remains. It stands—again—as a Highway 3 landmark.

The timeworn old pine continues to stop traffic. Its legacy lives on.

Active development of both the town and mine at Bellevue began in 1903, according to *The Crowsnest and Its People* (Crowsnest Pass Historical Society, 1979) and the "Historical Walking Tour of Bellevue" (Crowsnest Heritage Initiative pamphlet, 2010). Remarkably, Bellevue did not become incorporated as a village until 1957.

The village of Bellevue sprung up around the West Canadian Collieries Mine and was well developed by 1909. French-based West Canadian Collieries Ltd. began prospecting in the Pass in 1898. The collieries subsequently bought 20,000 acres of land that encompassed the future townsite of Lille, north of Bellevue in the Gold Creek Valley, and Blairmore to the west, along with Byron Creek to the south of town in 1903. In 1908, Bellevue's population increased significantly with the opening of Bellevue's second mine by Maple Leaf Collieries, southeast of the West Canadian Collieries Mine.

NOTE: Because the subject matter of this book deals mainly with historical events following World War II, earlier mining disasters in the Pass will not be covered in great detail.

The most notable accident was the Hillcrest Mine disaster of 1914, which claimed the lives of 189 people, the worst mining disaster in Canadian history. The Bellevue Mine Explosion of 1910 claimed 31 victims. Hundreds of miners lost their lives in mining accidents over the years, including my grandfather James Albert Radford. Most of the dead from the worst accidents were buried in mass graves.

My grandmother Victoria Sapeta used to tell me she dreaded the sound of the mine whistle, as did every wife in the Pass. Whistles signalled if there was work or if there had been a mining accident.

View of Turtle Mountain looking west, which probably led to the expression
"Quelle un belle vue" and Bellevue's namesake.

The first Bellevue mine manager and founder, French national Jules J. Fleutot's daughter Elise (referred to as Elsie, erroneously, in some records) is reputed to have said "Quelle un belle vue" after which the expression Bellevue (and town) was named. In English, this translates into "What a beautiful view." The view from Bellevue to the west really is spectacular, with the massive Turtle Mountain thrusting into the heavens. Actually, the Pass has some of the most picturesque scenery in all of Canada if not the world. Sadly, the scenery has been blighted over the years because of what some residents believe are loose land-use bylaws.

A key local landmark is the majestic Crowsnest Mountain, which is situated to the west and north of Coleman. There is no other mountain quite like it in Canada. Crowsnest Mountain and Chief Mountain to the south in Montana both arise from what is known as "klippe" geology, with older strata overlying younger rocks, the opposite of typical geological formations.

Crowsnest Mountain, with the Seven Sisters Peak in the background and Crowsnest Lake in the foreground.

The Crowsnest Pass is the most southerly of all three passes through the Canadian Rockies that are used by railways. The railroad is not used for transcontinental traffic. It was constructed in 1898 to develop the mining industry in Alberta and British Columbia.

The Pass was formerly one of the most important Canadian mining centres for producing coking coal and steam coal. Coal mining was the main industry from the early 1900s until the early 1960s. The discovery of oil at Leduc in 1947 and the Canadian Pacific Railway decision to convert its locomotives to burning diesel fuel were the major contributing factors to the fall in demand for coal. The first diesel locomotive-powered train arrived at Lethbridge in 1952. These key changes eliminated what was once a strong national and domestic market for coal.

On April 10, 1957, Bellevue Mine operations were suspended, putting 194 workers out of work. For the next four years, West Canadian Collieries merely monitored the Bellevue Mine as it continued to run the Grassy Mountain strip mine coal through the Bellevue Mine tipple. A "tipple" is an engineering structure used at a mine to load coal into railroad hopper cars. Grassy Mountain is located in the headwaters of Gold Creek. In 1961, the mine was permanently closed and the tipple removed in 1962, ending mining in Bellevue.

PEOPLE OF THE PASS

According to William Cousins, two large language groups consisting of white Europeans dominated the Pass towns prior to 1952. The Slavs—consisting of Russians, Poles, Ukrainians, Yugo-Slavs, Czechs, and Slovaks—were the largest group, while all the people originating from the British Isles, together with Americans and eastern Canadians, formed the other. Cousins noted that Italians formed a sizeable proportion of the population of all the towns. There were many other nationalities, and the census taker in Blairmore in 1941 found that there were at least thirty-three nationalities in that town alone, which would have been representative of the other towns. Cousins noted that following 1945, large numbers of displaced persons came to the Pass. The largest group of displaced persons consisted of veterans of General Ander's Polish army, which had disbanded in Italy.

Relatively few Chinese Canadians lived in the Pass after World War II, and those that did were primarily owners of Chinese restaurants and their families. These restaurants also had small confectionaries, which sold candy and cigarettes, along with other condiments. It was a real treat to eat in a restaurant during the fifties, which was an indulgence few families could afford. I have no recollection of ever eating meals with my family in any restaurants in the Pass, and neither did most of my friends, who were also too poor to eat out.

I first saw people of Japanese Canadian descent in my teens, when I played against a bantam rep hockey team from Lethbridge in a series of exhibition games. The Japanese Canadian boys on this team were very good hockey players, nifty skaters and excellent stick handlers with a high skill level. They were likely descendants of Japanese Canadian families who had been interned in camps during the World War II near Lethbridge under the War Measures Act. Families were offered the option of working on sugar beet farms in Alberta, which were common around Lethbridge, so they could stay together.

There were no people of black descent or what used to be called Indo-Canadians or other visible minorities now called "people of colour" in the Pass while I was growing up. Pass residents were predominantly white Europeans at the time.

I never heard of the term "racist" as a kid. I have no memories of any systemic racism at the time. However, at least some people believed there was an undercurrent of discrimination in the Pass in the 1950s. Discrimination was tied to nationalities, not races. Some people of British descent apparently thought they were better than anyone else; after all, the British Empire had basically conquered the world. The unflattering name "bohunk" was coined for Bohemians from the Czech Republic. This contemptuous name became "bohonk" in the Pass. Also common were racial slurs such as "Dago" for immigrants from Italy, Portugal, or Spain and "Polack" for Polish immigrants.

However, there was also a lot of tolerance. My father had a good relationship with people of all nationalities, many of whom would invite us into their homes for a glass of homemade wine or something else to drink after we delivered a load of coal. Although I was still a kid, I'd often be offered a glass of red wine, which I found rather dry. When "displaced people" from Europe arrived after World War II, they were talked about in hushed tones as being "DPs," which carried a certain stigma. I felt sorry for one Dutch family, the "Vinks," who settled in Bellevue about 1954. Classmates George and Peter Vink were noted by Mrs. Shafer as being "non-English" but remarkably were B students less than a year later and seemed to quickly transition to a Canadian lifestyle.

DAILY LIFE

There was a Royal Canadian Legion in Bellevue, Blairmore and Coleman, as the Pass had many veterans. Many social activities revolved around the legions, especially during the weekends, where the game of darts was always popular.

Alberta had segregated drinking halls for forty years. Between 1927 and 1967, drinking establishments were required to have separate entrances for "Ladies and Escorts" and "Men." My mom and dad often went to the Bellevue Legion on Saturday nights. The last serving would be at midnight, and consequently, many patrons would load their table with beer when the lights started to flash, signalling that the bar would close soon. My dad said there was one old soldier who once wrote a note on his table that he spit in his beer to stop other patrons from drinking it when he went to the toilet and left it unattended. Someone with a sense of humour added at the bottom of the note, "So did I."

Folks could call in a liquor order by telephone to the Alberta Liquor Control Board store in Blairmore and have free delivery of spirits. Popular local beer labels featured Lethbridge Brewing and Malting Company pilsner and Calgary Brewing and Malting Company ale, with the iconic buffalo head and horseshoe logo.

New vehicles were virtually unheard of after the end of World War II. They were out of the price range of most miners and sawmill employees, who struggled just to keep food on the table and coal in their sheds. The first time my father bought a new car was in the 1960s, a black Volkswagen beetle. Some of the senior mine officials were relatively well off financially. They seemed to be among the few townsfolk who could afford a new vehicle.

My uncle Bob Shevels, who married my dad's sister, Beth, bought a 1956 Chevrolet Bel Air, with a V8 motor; that was one of the first new vehicles I ever rode in. I can remember the power of the car as Uncle Bob drove up a steep hill on Highway 3 in drive gear after crossing the Oldman River, on our way to Pincher Creek. Most vehicles would have had to gear down to make the grade.

Many townsfolk eked out a subsistence existence, with men often living off unemployment insurance when out of work, while some families were on relief from the mine unions, which wasn't a lot of money. Some families also lived off welfare. It was not uncommon for men to be laid off in any of the coal mines or sawmills if there was a slump in demand for coal or when the weather was unsuitable to mill trees.

Discipline in the schools was very strict. Life was often tough. People lived in an environment with a lot of adversity that forged and hardened their character. When boys became teenagers, they were expected to work alongside adults and that's how they became men.

I don't recall the Pass having "considerable drinking and brawling" as described by Cousins in his book, *A History of the Crow's Nest Pass*. I would have been too young to remember much before 1952, where Cousins described many examples of widespread lawlessness. Granted, there were some fistfights between young men that were often associated with girls at school dances and the weekend dances held in Blairmore but not outright brawling. Each town had its own police force, or at least a constable. Zigmund Scropski was hired as Bellevue's first constable in 1958. My folks called him "Ziggy."

A friend of mine from America, Bob Henninger, who grew up in the same era as I did, related the following rites of passage that characterized our childhoods.

- Most of us had to earn our own money; it wasn't given to us!
- Good manners were not suggested, they were mandated— no exceptions.
- Elders were to be respected, not belittled.
- Charity and kindness were taught by example.
- Every kid was invited to birthday parties.
- Local police were respected and knew most kids by name in the neighbourhood.
- Kids were expected to open doors for others and give up their seats on buses and trolley cars to ladies and older people.
- Serving your country was honoured and respected. Veterans were venerated and admired for their service.
- Toys like baseball gloves, bats, footballs, even skates, and bikes were shared with those less fortunate.
- Most of us walked to school; some more than a mile and often further.
- Lunches were not free. You either walked home for lunch or carried it in a bag or lunch box. Peanut butter and jam were more common than anything else, with an apple or orange— never candy and seldom cookies.
- Weekends were for family chores; when you finished you were free to go out and play.
- The most dreaded words were, "When your father gets home . . ."
- Kids in unhappy situations "toughed it out." Suicides of children were extremely rare to almost nonexistent; now, the highest death rates over fatal diseases and other causes! What does that say about today's society and parenting?
- Finally, grandparents supported family rules with gentle wisdom and comfort.

It wasn't until after the towns (Blairmore and Coleman) and villages (Bellevue, Frank, and Hillcrest) in the Pass amalgamated as a Municipal District of Crowsnest Pass in 1979 that the Royal Canadian Mounted Police established a headquarters in Blairmore to police the Pass where the municipal government office was located.

After World War II until the early 1960s, most men in the Pass either worked in underground coal mines at Bellevue, Blairmore, and Coleman or at strip mines on the Adanac Summit, Grassy Mountain, Racehorse Creek, and Tent Mountain. The Burmis Lumber Company would have been another key industry in the Pass at the time. The underground miners had dangerous jobs, hauling mine props, shoring the mine shafts, and shovelling coal day long. Hauling coal by trucks from the strip mines was scary to say the least, especially during the winter. Local miners would take a bus to mines outside of their towns. My father told me many harrowing tales of hauling truckloads of coal on these snow-swept, slippery, and treacherous mountain roads.

Most of the merchants in the Pass depended on the coal mines and Burmis Lumber Company for their business. During the time of this story, Bellevue was a vibrant community, with a school, bank, bakery, barber shop, dairy, a dry goods and grocery store, a hardware story, bar and hotel, Chinese and Canadian restaurants, a couple of small garages and service stations, movie theatre, drugstore (i.e., pharmacy and confectionary), Royal Canadian Legion, two pool halls, hockey arena and curling rink, a shoemaker, Catholic and United Churches, and the Canada Post Office. However, it was not uncommon for men from nearby Hutterite colonies to come knocking on the door selling farm produce, especially chickens, geese, and fresh vegetables. During the 1950s, Bellevue had a population of about 1500. The population had shrunk to about 800 in 2006, the last year such statistics were available.

Beverley (Joanie) Amos in her figure skating outfit—1952
(Photo Credit: Dennis Amos).

There were few organized sports for kids, and most minor league hockey games were played as exhibition games, sometimes with impromptu playoffs for kids in bantam and midget leagues. Figure skating was in its beginnings at the time but was popular with girls, such as my adorable neighbour and babysitter, the late Beverley (Joan or Joanie) Amos, who passed away in 2020. Some teens enjoyed curling; my brother was a keen curler.

Few parents ever watched their kids play organized sports. Neither my mother nor father had ever attended a hockey game I played in, as compared to the idolized state of children's hockey nowadays. This wasn't isolated to just the Pass; it was fairly common elsewhere in

Alberta at the time. Hardly any players in town had new hockey equipment; most of mine was second hand, except for some hockey pants, while new hockey sticks were rare and all made of wood. I still remember my joy when my cousin-in-law Bill White gave me all his old hockey equipment. Bill was a good player and had played in local senior leagues. A hockey stick cost about $5 in the mid-1950s which was a lot of money back then. A day's wages for an adult might only be $10 at the time, if they could find work. The only standard garment was the team jerseys; socks and pants were a mismatch of styles and colours held in place with rubber quart sealers.

There were few places to get hockey skates sharpened outside of local rinks, which weren't always open when you needed to get them sharpened. Sometimes, I resorted to using one of my dad's metal files to sharpen them, which didn't work very well because the blades are supposed to be hollow ground with a ridge on either side of the blade.

There were no Zamboni ice machines in any arena in the Pass. Rink rats (i.e., young kids) hand-swept snow off the ice with push brooms while the ice was flooded by hand after games with a con-traption made from a forty-five-gallon drum. The local arenas were popular for skating during the long winters, and there was a curling rink in the same building in the rinks in Bellevue and Blairmore. The Bellevue rink has been long demolished and replaced with a park and playground.

While playing billiards was common in one of the two pool halls in Bellevue, going to a movie in the local theatre was also a favou-rite local pastime. The cost of admission for a Saturday afternoon matinee at the Rex Theatre in Bellevue was $0.15, and either a pop or bag of popcorn cost $0.10. If there was a good movie, my friends and I would try to get there early enough to get our hand on the door handle so we were first inside.

Most kids participated in outdoor activities all year round, seldom doing anything in their homes except playing card games and monopoly or watching television shows. There were no such things as video games or cell phones; the internet was but a dream. My old neighbour, Allan (Chuck) Amos, sent me the following song, epitomizing what our childhoods were like back in the day.

COAL TOWN KIDS by Allan (Chuck) Amos

Down the hill and across the tracks, over the bridge to the old
    coal slack
Past the big pine tree and thru the fence to Maloff's land
With a slingshot or twenty-two, we'd shoot anything that moved
Back then that was something we just loved to do

Chorus
A kid's life was pretty easy, growing up in our little coal town
Our folks worked hard to make it that way; I know they sacrificed
To give us a better life; I'll remember that until my dying day
We'd stock up at Joe's Café for the Saturday matinee
Then head on down and wait to get inside, fifteen cents to see
    the show, ten cents that we could blow on anything our little
    hearts desired

Solo
I remember still how we rode our bikes to Lille
And all of those big hills we had to climb; we packed lunch for
    the day
And drank from streams along the way, if we made it home by five
    everything was okay

Chorus

A kid's life was pretty easy, growing up in our little coal town
Our folks worked hard to make it that way; I know they sacrificed
To give us a better life; I'll remember that until my dying day
We'd stock up at Joe's Café for the Saturday matinee

Then head on down and wait to get inside, fifteen cents to see
    the show, ten cents that we could blow on anything our little
    hearts desired

We'd ride the bull barrel in the stall, and high mark on the wall
But no matter how we tried Jim always won
Thinking back to those coal town days, there's one thing for sure
    I'll say
None of us had money, but we sure had fun

Winters in the Pass were usually brutal throughout the 1950s, with deep snow and bitter cold. Winds, often fierce, would create huge snow drifts, with -20°F (the standard measure of temperatures of the day) not being uncommon during January and February. Roads were seldom plowed unless there was a major snowstorm, so walking to and from school was often a challenge. Practically nobody had a paved driveway or side walk; driveways had to be hand-shovelled with banjo coal shovels after big storms, which often took the better part of a day. It was not uncommon for snow drifts to be five to six feet deep in the driveway of Ted Amos, our next-door neighbour. It was only neighbourly to help shovel out a neighbour's driveway, and this was usually delegated to children.

The Pass often experienced Chinook winds that could result in a temperature change all the way from -20°F to +5°F overnight. It was entirely normal for our house to shake during the strong winds that were prevalent each spring and autumn. On one occasion during the fall, wind gusts exceeded 100 mph and tore the roof off homes and buildings, shattered windows, and lifted sheds off their foundations, carrying them skyward. The wind was so strong, it picked up gravel off the roads and pelted me and my friends as we played in railway cars beside the Bellevue Mine, near our home. The surrounding countryside also experienced a few severe blow-downs from time to time. These blow-downs snapped coniferous trees off the ground in the nearby mountains, some with two-foot butts, flattening everything in their path. Two of the worst blow-downs happened in Tent Mountain Pass, which borders British Columbia south of Sentinel and Caudron Creek in the Gold Creek Valley, north of the Frank Slide.

June 22 is the date of my birthday. It invariably rained on every one of my birthdays until I left the Pass. The weather could be awful and was erratic; strong winds, cold winters with deep snow, and sheets of rain in the spring were the norm.

THE BURMIS LUMBER COMPANY BY TONY STOKLOSA

For those of us whom wished to find employment other than that in a coal mine, we were fortunate to have a secondary industry supporting our community. The logging industry was dominated by the Burmis Lumber Company, which had a lumber mill twenty-five miles south of Hillcrest. Here, raw logs were cut and processed into rough lumber, which was transported to the planner mill at Burmis, located between Highway 3 and the CPR rail track. Being close to a railhead gave great opportunity to market local lumber beyond our borders.

My first job at the Bush Mill, at age seventeen, was that of choker/ swamper. Once the tree faller dropped a tree, the swamper's job was to de-limb the tree using a double-bladed axe. Any limbs four to five inches long were cut off with a chainsaw by the faller. Then came the attachment of a twenty-foot, three-quarter-inch steel cable, with a hook on one end and a loop on the other. A D7 Caterpillar driver came up close, pushing something on two large tires called an "arch." This contraption had a metal gooseneck-type protrusion with rollers and supported a cable with a large hook. We would hook the "choker" around the butt of the log, slip the hook back around the cable, then place the looped end onto a large hook of the arch.

When we had six or seven trees choked, the cat operator would winch up the logs tight to the arch gooseneck and proceed to drag them to the mill about a half to one mile away. There, they were dropped at a "landing," unchoked, then bucked up into standard lengths of eight, ten, or twelve feet, and so on. These chunks were then sent up a mobile steel ladder and put under high pressure water for cleanup before entering the mill to be sawed up into boards.

If we felt the choking and swamping was too tough or dangerous, we were encouraged to say so. Then we were given another task, such as piling the cut lumber boards into respective stacks of eight, ten, or twelve feet and so on, off the "green chain." When complete, each separate pile was picked up by truck and hauled to Burmis Planner Mill for the finished product.

Both labour tasks mentioned above were just too much for me, as I was small of stature and not as tough as the likes of George Dowson, Frankie Toborski, Bob Storey, and Victor Belick. An opportunity presented itself when I was approached by the mill's foreman, John Wanagut. He was looking for someone with mathematical skills to work inside the mill, taking on the job of a "timber scaler." This work entailed estimating the board feet of the log before being sawed up. I claimed I could add, subtract, divide, and document better than most, so Mr. Wanagut said, "Your hired." Phew, for a second, I thought he said, "You're fired!"

Once the log was entered into the mill, my job was to stop its movement on the "jack ladder" by use of a brake lever. Then with a four-foot measuring stick, which had a brass T on one end, I measured the diameter at the wide end, multiplied it by its length, then subtracted or discounted my estimation of imperfection or waste to come up with a figure of board feet of usable lumber. This figure was then transferred onto a tally sheet. At the end of the shift, I added up all the tallied logs and entered the estimated number of board feet in the total box. Each log was flipped off its mooring using a "cant hook" or peavey, then rolled down a ramp to the sawing carriage. The daily tally sheet was taken at shift's end to the commissary shack, where the accountant, Mr. Stevens, logged it and others into the accounting books.

Once a week, my daily tally sheets were compared to the tally at the planner mill. My estimates were so accurate that three weeks into the job, Mr. Wanagut gave me a raise of $0.10 an hour to $1.96 per hour. Yikes, I was getting rich, and this was also why I kept at the job for two summer seasons. By the time I resigned my employ to head to the big city for other opportunities, I was toughened, trim, and slim from flipping logs, not to mention had sixteen-inch biceps.

I have to mention how some of us travelled to that lumber mill at Lost Creek. One of the company mechanics, Frank Hill, lived in Bellevue. He drove his half-ton truck over the Adanac Road daily and would pick us up at Hillcrest. Two lads sat in the cab with the driver, and two or three sat huddled in the open box behind the cab. [Author's Note: See Jim Jepson's story "Coal Town Boys."] Thank God for those oversized army surplus parkas we were able to purchase, as I am certain we would have frozen to death as we drove in -30°C winter weather to the Bush camp. After a few months of this, I made the decision to head to the city and look for a warm, inside job.

SHOOT-OUT AT JOE'S CAFÉ

Although the following story pre-dates my childhood, it's worth telling because it represents one of the most memorable, infamous events in the history of Bellevue if not Canada.

Beside the long-standing Bellevue Inn on what is now the main street in town is the Bellevue Café. During my youth, the Bellevue Café was a favourite hang-out for school kids, and it was known as Jim's Café and earlier it was named after his father, Joe's Café.

The proprietor, Jim Mah (Joe's son) made delicious hamburgers that he topped with crisp, grilled Spanish onions. I asked Jim what the secret was for his famous burgers. He said all he did was cook them after sprinkling salt on a grill, without using any butter or vegetable oil. His thick and creamy milkshakes were also a treat. I bought my first package of cigarettes there: Players filter. Jim stood behind the counter, looking askance, shifting his feet. He slowly shook his head sideways, inquiring if they were for me, as I was only about fourteen years old at the time, even though minors could smoke. I think I might have told him a white lie and said I was buying them for my father, who actually smoked Players plain, no filter. Most often, I'd buy Marlboro Menthol filter tip cigarettes, which I thought might be better for my health. Go figure. At the time, smoking was still considered cool. You couldn't fool Jim, who knew all the local kids by their first name. In 1975, Jim moved to Calgary and opened the Phoenix Inn Restaurant in the downtown area after business dropped off when the local mines closed.

Dennis Amos beside a Mustang (circa 1965) in front of Jim's Café, aka Joe's Café or the Bellevue Café (Photo Credit: Dennis Amos).

The Bellevue Café still looks pretty much as it did on the momentous Saturday morning of August 7, 1920. On August 2, 1920, three local migrant Russian miners—George Arkoff, Ausby Auloff, and Tom Bassoff—robbed the passengers of the Canadian Pacific Railway's train No. 63 at gunpoint. They'd hoped to find wealthy rum-runner Emilio "Emperor Pic" Picariello aboard. Rumour had it that Pic was carrying $10,000 in cash to buy liquor. Prohibition of liquor sales in Alberta became law on July 1, 1916. Prohibition lasted until May 10, 1924.

For some reason, Pic got off the train early, so the robbers ended up stealing what they could from the remaining passengers, making off with about $300 to $400 (various sources report differing amounts were stolen) and some jewellery. After the robbery, they eluded the Royal Canadian Mounted Police (RCMP), the Alberta Provincial Police (APP), and the Canadian Pacific Railway Police. Auloff escaped into the United States while Bassoff and Arkoff remained in the Pass.

On August 7, these two bandits were spotted in Joe's Bellevue Café. Three constables entered the café through the front and back doors. In an ensuing shoot-out, Arkoff, RCMP Constable Ernest Usher, and APP Constable F. W. E. Bailey were killed. Newspaper reports claimed that it was Bassoff, himself, who put a final bullet in the head of his accomplice, Arkoff, to put him out of his misery, who'd been wounded by the police and lay on the street outside the café. Bassoff, though wounded in his legs, escaped into the rubble of the Frank Slide. During the pursuit, Special Constable Nicolas Kyslik was accidentally shot and killed by another officer. Bassoff was eventually apprehended without incident on August 11, 1920, at Pincher Station, thirty-five kilometres east of Bellevue.

Although testimony suggests that the police officers had failed to identify themselves and had probably fired first, Bassoff was found guilty of murder and hanged in Lethbridge, Alberta, on December 22, 1920. Justice was swift back in the day. Ausby Auloff was eventually captured in 1924 near Butte, Montana, after trying to sell a distinctive railway watch. Auloff, who had not been involved in the shoot-out, was returned to Alberta, where he was sentenced to seven years imprisonment. He died in 1926.

The tale has been immortalized in the following poem, although a variation of actual events that Allan (Chuck) Amos sent me, which many locals knew by heart.

The Shoot-out at the Bellevue Café (Author Unknown)

When Bassoff came to Bellevue to rob the Union Bank
He walked into the Bellevue Café and in a chair he sank.
He ordered beef and onions and apple pie for two.

He slung a piece to Arkoff, his pal, so good and true.
When the police heard Bassoff was in town
They filled their pockets full of lead, walked into the Bellevue Café
    and said,
"Bassoff, you're under arrest in the name of the Queen."

But Bassoff was a sly old mutt; he shot from 'neath the table
And plugged one in the gut.
Some ran around the corners, afraid of being hit
While others stood as paralysed and filled their pants.

In December 1989, the Bellevue Café was designated as a registered historic resource by Alberta Culture. The original clapboard siding and window details of the front elevation were reconstructed in 1990 by the Alberta Main Street Program. At press time, the infamous café was on the market for $224,900.

THE FRANK SLIDE

This book would not be complete without mentioning the Frank Slide, where at least ninety people lost their lives in 1903. In its own way, the slide, Canada's worst natural disaster, has always been shrine for residents of the Pass, a grim reminder of the many disasters the area has experienced.

Oral history of the local Blackfoot and Ktunaxa Indigenous peoples, whose traditional lands encompassed the Pass, referred to Turtle Mountain as "the mountain that moves." They were frightened of a landslide, and it's said that they did not camp in at the base of the mountain for fear it would fall.

The slide has been designated as a Provincial Historic Site of Alberta. Even though this event is the most spectacular natural disaster in the history of Canada, many locals probably took the slide for granted.

Turtle Mountain (L) and the Frank Slide (centre) the focal point of the Crow's Nest Pass, with Highway 3 in the centre of the picture.

The mountain's limestone summit fractured and cascaded downhill, covering the Canadian Pacific Railway tracks and obliterating most of the Frank townsite in about ninety seconds. The area was covered by shattered limestone rock several square miles in area. Some of the slide rocks are the size of houses, literally.

Every morning in the Pass, I'd wake up to a panoramic view of Turtle Mountain from our kitchen window in Bellevue. From Grade 9 to 11, I took a school bus through the slide from Bellevue to Blairmore. It was always an awesome site and sad to see so many people painting the slide rocks with graffiti, dishonouring people who lost their lives in the slide. Over time, people made a few short walking trails into the slide rock, which was largely impenetrable.

As kids, my friends and I would walk along the railway tracks that traversed the slide, looking for fallen or lost booty from passing trains. You'd be surprised at what we'd find—lost tools, flares, spikes, and so on. We'd put our ears down on the tracks to listen for the hum of approaching trains to stay clear of them when they passed.

The slide rocks were mined by the Canadian Pacific Railway for road-grade ballast. Local highway contractors also used slide rock as a source of rock to armour roads that might be in danger of being washed out by streams.

The slide was a huge obstacle for local traffic. Even after Highway 3 had been upgraded, it could be a treacherous stretch of road. It would ice over during the winter and could be very slippery. I recall my mother losing control of our car on a Sunday afternoon one winter on an icy patch of road and sliding into the ditch. The kids were in the back seat, which certainly added to the excitement of a trip to our grandparents in Coleman. In those days, cars did not have power steering or power brakes and tires did not have the traction they do today. On another occasion, while my brother was driving our dad's car, its hood sprung open in the middle of the slide during a severe windstorm and blocked our view of the road; fortunately, Jimmy managed to slow the car down and pull it over to the ditch, where we jury-rigged the latch on the hood.

A lot of non-locals did not know that there was a dusty, rough secondary road to the south of Highway 3 through the slide that paralleled the Crowsnest River. The old Frank Road was built through the debris field of the Frank Slide in 1917. There were hidden trails along the old road beside Gold Creek that led down to the river. Local anglers would take this road to go fishing in the Crowsnest River and in Frank Lake, which wasn't actually a lake but rather a widening of the river.

Over time, Frank Lake has largely filled in with sediment and is only a fraction of the size it was when I was growing up. Frank Lake was also a popular destination of local kids, who would make wooden rafts to get around this slow-moving part of the river. None of the ones I recall were safe, and it's a small miracle that nobody drowned. The few that I tried were all tippy—one wrong move and you'd be in the water. On the north side of this road near some abandoned lime kilns there was a small pond hidden from the dirt road where you could sometimes shoot ducks during the autumn migration. Some winters my friends and I would use the pond for games of shinny, lighting a bonfire on the shore to keep warm. Because of the strong winds the pond would often be clear of snow and fine for skating.

The Bellevue dump was located on the northeast corner of the slide just off Highway 3. This is where my dad hauled garbage from the town. It was a filthy, stinky landfill, where people dumped all manner of garbage, including waste from septic tanks. We often saw black bears rummaging around in the dump whenever we visited there. Nobody paid any attention to what amounted to desecration of a major historic site.

At the end of school in June, our Bellevue Elementary School teachers would often lead the children on an outing along the northern fringe of the slide rocks, on an old road, to the ghost town of Lille, where we'd have a picnic to celebrate the end of the school year. Some late blooming shooting stars and yellow-bell flowers might've still been flowering to brighten the day; perhaps a few lingering prairie crocuses (pasqueflowers) might also have been in flower. Schools did not host trips for students to foreign countries or elsewhere even in Alberta; people were frugal and could not even think about such luxuries. It was hard enough just to leave the Pass for a short vacation.

Although I've hiked all along the top of the Livingstone Range, as far north as Centre Peak, I never made it to the top of Turtle Mountain. The one time my neighbour Dennis Amos and his cousin Larry Svoboda and I attempted to scale the peak on a hot summer day, we stopped short of the summit. We headed up on the Hillcrest side, the worst approach, and were blocked by cliffs. If we'd targeted our climb a bit further south, we would have been able to bypass them. There is a well-used trail up the backside of Turtle Mountain starting in Blairmore that is a much easier hike.

2
FAMILY LIFE

DAD AND MOM

Carrie and Sam Radford, circa 1943.

The story of my parents is probably like those of many Pass pioneers and bears telling for that reason. My father, Samuel Owen Radford, was born in Bellevue on February 7, 1915, and grew up in the Dairy area north of Main Street. He passed away of cancer in Calgary on December 30, 1969, at age fifty-four. This was before the days of chemo therapy, and the only form of cancer treatment was radium if I recall correctly, which many believed was so damaging as to be of little value. The first four children in his family were born in Springhill, Nova Scotia: Beth, Beatrice, Doris, and James. Jessie, Sam(uel), and Fred were born in Bellevue.

My mother, Caroline Ann Sapeta, was born in Coleman on December 8, 1914. She passed away in Calgary on September 10, 2013, at age ninety-nine. Grandma called her "Carola" in Polish; otherwise, she was usually called Carrie, seldom Caroline. She was raised in Bushtown, in southeast Coleman, within a stone's throw of the Crowsnest River. There were ten children in her family; three died as infants and one daughter, Jennie, at the age of six, of appendicitis, which killed a lot of people back in the day. Those born and raised in Coleman were Alice, Helen, Carl, Carrie, Joe, and Violet. High rates of infant mortality were not uncommon prior to World War II.

My mother and father were married in Lethbridge on September 27, 1941. The attendants were Mr. and Mrs. Stuart (Helen) Newton; Helen was my mother's sister. They went on a brief honeymoon in Calgary. Big fancy weddings were virtually unheard of at the time. There were no so-called "destination weddings," which would have been unheard of. My brother, James (Jim or Jimmy) Albert was born on January 18, 1944, in Vancouver, and now resides in Edmonton with his wife, Betty. I was born on June 22, 1946, in Blairmore. My middle name is Samuel after my dad's first name. My sister, Jill Casa, was born on August 7, 1952, in Blairmore. She now resides on an acreage with her husband, Ray Bussey, near Springbank, Alberta. The letters "Ca" in her middle name stands for Caroline and "sa" for Samuel.

Carrie and Sam Radford (circa 1943), location unknown.

My father and mother were both high school graduates, a rarity at the time; not many people completed high school, with most leaving school as soon as they reached Grade 9. My mother finished at the top of her class in Grade 12 and, subsequently, attended Garbutt's Business College in Calgary. She attended college with a friend from Coleman, Alma Hedberg. As the top student from the Coleman High School, my mother had won a free trip to Poland sponsored by the local Polish benevolent society, which her father wisely advised her to forego because World War II was on the horizon. The second highest-ranking student took the trip and never returned. Nobody knew what happened to her; she simply vanished into Nazi occupied Europe.

After my mother graduated from Garbutt's Business College, she worked as a stenographer for five years at Joe D'Appolonia's Excel Builders, a Coleman building contractor, before her marriage. After graduating from high school, my father worked for Bellevue Collieries as a coal miner. He enlisted in the Royal Canadian Navy on June 17, 1942, in Calgary at the age of twenty-seven as an electrician and transferred to the Photographic Branch on August 5, 1942. His brother, Fred, enlisted in the Royal Canadian Air Force.

My father served in the Royal Canadian Navy from May 2, 1942, until his discharge on August 2, 1945, for approximately thirty-seven months service ashore in Canada. He seldom talked to me about his service in World War II, although he said training stints on Corvettes were enough to make even the best sailors seasick. He was initially stationed in Halifax before transferring to Vancouver. His Naval Training and Active Service records show "No Sea Time." He achieved the rank of chief petty officer by the end of the war. A chief petty officer is the most senior non-commissioned member rank of the Royal Canadian Navy. It is equivalent to a chief warrant officer in the Canadian Army and Royal Canadian Air Force.

Bellevue Transfer Company trucks (circa 1950) from my dad's trucking company.

Following the war, he worked as a partner with John(ny) Raymaker in the Bellevue Transfer Company, a small trucking business, mainly hauling coal. He bought out Johnny in 1959 and became the sole owner of the trucking company until it was sold in 1964. He had a garbage removal contract with the town of Bellevue, which also involved picking up ashes from coal furnace. The transfer company was also engaged with pumping cesspools, moving furniture, and doing whatever helped pay the bills.

My dad was a member of the Royal Canadian Legion, the Masonic Lodge, and the first chief of the volunteer Bellevue Fire Department. I can remember being banished to my room when he got dressed for Masonic Lodge meetings in conformity with their dress code, which was secret back in the day. He said it was essential to belong to the Masonic Lodge if you wanted to do any business in the Crowsnest Pass; otherwise, you'd be blackballed by the local businessmen.

The volunteer Bellevue Fire Department, formed 1951: Pictured in the photo are members of the brigade kneeling in the foreground of their newly remodelled fire engine: George K. Sirett, Fire Chief Sam Radford, Assistant Chief Jack Giolo, Ernest Goulding, Joe Fortunaso, John Paul, Secretary Les Cousins, Louis Olinek, Bill Gregory, Robert Glover, Jim Svoboda, and Lawrence Rosio (L–R). One member of the fire department, Cecil Singleton, was not present (supplied).

The Bellevue Fire Department was formed in 1951 and held practices every Wednesday, weather permitting. The brigade had twelve men. They participated in an annual Hose Coupling Competition held in Coleman each July 1 (Canada Day) and were regarded as a crack team. Once a year, the brigade held its firemen's ball at New Year's Eve; at Halloween, the members also had a banquet.

While most fire-fighting duties took place in Bellevue, they were also called to fight fires in rural areas outside the village limits. On one occasion, they were called to put out a fire on a frigid winter night at the Lundbreck Hotel, which burned to the ground. My dad told me that their "pumper-truck" ran out of water and they had to use a cesspool as a source of "water" to fight the fire. On another occasion, a fire broke out after the Halloween Firemen's Ball in October 1953 at the Hillcrest-Mohawk Tipple (formerly called the Maple Leaf Mine) beside Highway 3. The fire was within eyesight of our home. There was a big party at our house that night after the firemen's ball, a big deal back in the day. I can still remember the flames shooting into the sky. What a spectacle! All the volunteer firemen had to abandon our house party to fight the fire that gutted the tipple, rats, to the consternation of their spouses!

EARLY YEARS IN MY BELLEVUE HOME

I was born in a four-room midwifery home in Blairmore and grew up in Bellevue. At the time, most children were born in midwifery homes, not hospitals. Our house in Bellevue was moved on a flatbed truck from Lille, I believe, in 1941. It was situated on a hillside lot on the southern edge of town, with a great view of the Crowsnest River from the living room.

Lille was the site of a coal mine in the Gold Creek Valley that was abandoned in 1912 and became a ghost town. William James Cousins wrote that "although some of the houses were taken away as soon as the mine closed, many buildings were left for many years." I can remember the spooky ruins of some homes and buildings that remained standing in the 1950s.

The house is unpainted in an early photo, dated 1941, and looks rather dingy. Although it would have been a bungalow at Lille, it became a two-story house in Bellevue. It featured a wooden veranda along the west and south side of the house. There was a wooden staircase to the veranda on the west side of the house, leading to a side door used as the main entry. I always found it odd that there was a front door off the veranda on the south side of the house; it that would have made sense in Lille but not in Bellevue. The upper level consisted of an unheated mudroom off the side entrance, which was called a "porch," kitchen, inside bathroom, living room, and two upstairs bedrooms. There was a garage in the basement, along with another bedroom with very poor heating, a small unheated pantry, coal room, coal furnace, utility room, small work shop, and an unfinished cement-walled shower.

Exterior of Sam and Carrie Radford's family home in Bellevue (circa 1941), moved from Lille.

The coal furnace had to be well stoked to keep the house warm. It was not unusual for the fire to go out overnight. We'd wake up to a cold house. It was so cold in the bedroom in the basement, you'd be able to see your breath. I recall sleeping on the couch in our living room as a teenager because it was too cold in my room in the basement.

My mother had a wringer washing machine in the utility room. She'd wash the clothes, then put them through the ringer to squeeze as much water out of them as possible before they went on a clothes-line—no small job. Monday was wash day, and if the temperature was above freezing, the clothes would be hung on a clothesline outside the house to dry. If it was below freezing, the clothes would be hung to dry inside the utility room on a series of clotheslines. Fortunately, our house was located upwind from the Bellevue Mine, so we were not plagued with dust from the mine that would settle on the wash, as happened in Maple Leaf, downwind of the mine site.

My dad would use the basement shower to get cleaned up after coming home from a day's work before he came upstairs into the mudroom and enter the kitchen. He would almost always be covered in coal dust or coal ashes from a day's work. I can still vividly remember all the crickets that used to live in the shower, which gave me the creeps.

Our pantry was a nirvana for mice during every season of the year; you couldn't keep them out of the house, and they'd always find their way inside under the garage doors.

The following missive and poem about rules for clotheslines describe what our mothers would do on wash day, usually Monday, regardless of the weather.

The Basic Rules for Clotheslines

1. *Hang the socks by the toes . . . NOT the top.*

2. *Hang pants by the BOTTOM or cuffs . . . NOT the waistbands.*

3. *WASH the clothesline(s) before hanging any clothes by walking the entire length of each line and holding a damp cloth around the lines.*

4. *Hang the clothes in the order: whites first, then coloured, and then darks.*

5. *NEVER hang a shirt by the shoulders, always by the tail! Because what would the neighbours think?*

6. *Wash day is Monday! NEVER hang clothes on the weekend, especially on Sunday, for heaven's sake!*

7. *Hang the sheets and towels on the OUTSIDE lines so you could hide your "unmentionables" in the middle.*

8. *It doesn't matter if it's sub-zero weather . . . clothes will "freeze-dry."*

9. *ALWAYS gather the clothespins when taking down dry clothes! Pins left on the lines were seen as "tacky."*

10. *Line clothes up so that each item does not need two clothespins but shares a clothespin with the next washed item.*

11. *Clothes should be off the line and neatly folded in the clothes basket before supper time and ready to be ironed.*

12. *Use a clothes pole (a long wooden pole) to push the middle of the clothesline up so that longer items (sheets/pants/etc.) don't brush the ground and get dirty.*

A CLOTHESLINE by Marilyn K. Walker

A clothesline was a news forecast
To neighbours passing by;
There were no secrets you could keep
When clothes were hung to dry.

It also was a friendly link for neighbours always knew
If company had stopped on by to spend a night or two.
For then you'd see the "fancy sheets" and towels upon the line;
You'd see the "company table cloths" with intricate designs.

The line announced a baby's birth,
From folks who lived inside,
As brand-new infant clothes were hung,
So carefully with pride!

The ages of the children could
So readily be known;
By watching how the sizes changed,
You'd know how much they'd grown!

It also told when illness struck,
As extra sheets were hung;
Then nightclothes, and a bathrobe too,
Haphazardly were strung.

It also said, "On vacation now,"
When lines hung limp and bare;
It told, "We're back!" when full lines sagged,
With not an inch to spare!

New folks in town were scorned upon
If wash was dingy and grey,
As neighbours carefully raised their brows,
And looked the other way.

But clotheslines now are of the past,
For dryers make work much less.
Now what goes on inside a home
Is anybody's guess!

I really miss that way of life,
It was a friendly sign;
When neighbours knew each other best
By what hung on the line.

Our house was situated on a large steeply sloped, gravelly lot on the southern edge of town and had a bird's-eye view of the Crowsnest River and Turtle Mountain. The lot was fenced in with a gate on the west side of the property that led to a path for trips uptown. Most of the yard was unkempt because of the steep terrain. It was impossible to keep weeds out.

There was a fairly large garden on the southern part of the lot on the west side of a driveway. Most families had a garden because they couldn't afford the luxury of store-bought vegetables. Root vegetables would generally be kept over-winter in cellars, although some were preserved in jars, for example beets and carrots.

On the other side of the driveway, there was a grassy area with an outside fireplace and what went for a patio. One of my chores was to try to keep the yard clean and tidy and cut the grass, using a hand sickle and push mower. Because of the steep slope of the yard, it was practically impossible to make it look very appealing. I still have bad dreams about the impossible job of trying to cut the grass and keep the yard in shape—a near hopeless task. The house is now owned by a family from Calgary that use it as a vacation property.

The Bellevue Coal Mine was located about half a mile away from our house, alongside the Canadian Pacific Railway tracks near the Crowsnest River. Several trains went through the Pass daily. The sound of train whistles was common, as were the sounds of railcars coupling and uncoupling during all hours of the day and night. Noise and racket from mine operations was a constant. Miners were forever hauling waste coal to dumps beside the Crowsnest River. It really was criminal what the miners did to the ecology of the Crowsnest River. I saw them dump truck loads of slack coal slurry into it many times. After a rainstorm, it would run black for days on end with coal fines, but nobody so much as raised an eyebrow. The Bellevue Mine closed in 1957, but this didn't signal the end of the town because the tipple was still used to process coal from the Grassy Mountain open-pit mine. The tipple was decommissioned in 1962 after the Grassy Mountain Mine ceased operating.

Virtually, all married women were stay-at-home housewives, my mother included. Their main job was looking after their households and raising children. Being a housewife was a full-time job: caring for the home, tending the garden, washing and drying clothes, and keeping furnaces stoked so water pipes didn't freeze. As a kid, one of my chores was to tend the furnace, stoking it with coal, emptying the furnace ashes, and starting the fire when it went out.

Most children went to elementary schools in each town. They walked to school, often returning home for lunch before returning to afternoon classes. It wasn't until Grade 7 that I started taking a school bus to a junior high school in nearby Hillcrest, then Maple Leaf in Bellevue, and later the Isabelle Sellon School in Blairmore.

Our big meal of the day was generally during the noon hour when my dad would take a break from work. Working men went through a lot of calories while doing physical labour all day. Usually a smaller meal would be served at supper except on Sunday when a large dinner would be the norm, often a traditional English roast beef with Yorkshire puddings. As my mother was Catholic, fish would always be on the menu each Friday, usually cod, halibut, or sole. It was customary for Catholics to eat fish on Friday at the time. Locally caught trout and mountain whitefish were always prized table fare.

Few homes had a deep freeze, so shopping was often a daily part of the family routine. The only family who had a freezer that I recall was Ted and Sally Amos's, our next-door neighbours. Fresh vegetables were scarce, especially during the winter, so many families canned garden vegetables or made their own preserves. Any kind of fruit was a real treat in our family and usually consisted of apples and oranges. Almost all families had a garden and cellar to store the vegetables and canned fruit and vegetables.

Being of British descent, my dad enjoyed eating traditional fare, such as pickled pigs' feet, kippered herrings, and blood sausage—all of which I found revolting. The smell of the herrings being cooked on a stovetop was enough to make me gag. I absolutely did not develop a taste for blood sausage, as I regarded it as rather barbaric fare. Pickled pigs' feet are usually salted and smoked, like ham and bacon. They are generally high in fat, and most people eat them as a snack, but I've never understood this, as I still find them revolting.

Kippered herrings are small, oily fish that have been butterflied dorsally from head to tail, then gutted, salted or pickled, and cold smoked, often over oak woodchips. While they're routinely eaten for breakfast in the United Kingdom, they were apparently once enjoyed during high tea or as a supper treat. My mother used to steam them in a skillet, which would usually drive everyone but my father from the kitchen, what with their awful odour.

Blood sausages have got to be some kind of throwback to the Neanderthal ages and are hardly appetizing. They're sausages filled with blood that my mother used to boil or grill in a skillet until they were done. It was all I could do to just taste them without gagging. To say that the Brits have peculiar eating habits is an understatement.

Because my father had a steady job, we were fortunate in being able to have food on the table—a luxury not all families could afford when miners were out of work. If my dad had a problem, it was that a lot of people were too poor to pay their bills. Lots of families ate Spam on a regular basis—in sandwiches, fried with potatoes, and so on.

A lot of people smoked cigarettes, not so much pipes, and the odd one, like my grandfather, White Owl cigars. It was rare not to see Papa without a cigar in his mouth. Cigarettes were cheap but still too expensive for lots of people, who rolled their own cigarettes. My aunts Alice Newton and Helen Williams both rolled their own smokes with canned tobacco and cigarette paper, as did a lot of other people. At the time, nobody knew that cigarettes caused lung cancer and other cancers.

In the early 1950s, inside bathrooms were uncommon in Bellevue or elsewhere in the Pass. In fact, most homes did not get inside plumbing until the late 1950s or early 1960s. Lots of houses in the Pass had outhouses, which could be especially challenging to use in the winter. My Sapeta grandparents had what's called a "two-seater" in their backyard. Not every home had an inside bathtub, and showers were rare. In some neighborhood homes, Friday or Saturday evening was bath night, when the whole family would bathe in a large galvanized tub, hand-filled with hot water heated on a coal stove. "The youngest family members would go first, up to the oldest," said Marilyn Costigan (nee Svoboda).

Fortunately, for our family, we had inside plumbing. There was an electric range in our kitchen that was a luxury at the time. By comparison, until the 1960s, my grandparents in Coleman used a coal stove for cooking, which also kept the house warm, along with a pot-belly stove in the living room they fired up during the winter months.

Sister Jill Radford beside Sylvania black and white TV set.

The first television broadcasts started in Canada in 1952 and soon became the most popular form of home entertainment for many families. I can still remember how proud my dad was when he purchased a Sylvania cabinet television, a top-of-the-line model at the time. The problem was TV signals were broadcast by microwave, and there was poor reception in the Pass. I would spend literally hours moving the antenna around our yard, trying to get decent reception on the black-and-white screen with the signature Indian-head test pattern. It wasn't until a new microwave tower was installed in Phillipps Pass, near Crowsnest Lake, that we got more reliable coverage. We'd also wrap aluminum foil around rabbit ears to ease the "snow" (i.e., blurry, stray signals) on the television screen. You could buy a type of pink or blue plastic wrap to minimize the "snow" and create the illusion of a colour television. While there were rumours that colour television was a coming invention, nobody actually believed such prophesies.

In the 1950s, family life started to revolve around American and Canadian television programs, with some of the most popular American series being *The Ed Sullivan Show* on Sunday night, *Father Knows Best,* and *Gunsmoke*, along with Canadian programs, such as *Hockey Night in Canada* on Saturday night, *Front Page Challenge*, and *The Wayne & Shuster Show.*

The Ed Sullivan Show was TV's longest-running variety show, spanning an unbelievable twenty-four seasons. Sullivan was characteristically a deadpan host, whose show featured the top entertainers of the day, although there were some corny acts. He was a strait-laced moderator who usually appeared to be a bit nervous. Celebrity singers, comedians, and entertainers were the feature stars.

I can still remember when Britain's famous rock stars the Beatles made an appearance to the delight of the crowd, where fans went wild. At the time, the Beatles had what many parents considered outrageously long hair, which was actually quite short by today's standards. Over the years, the Beatle's hairstyle became a bit dishevelled and longer, and they graduated from wearing suits to bizarre costumes, but the theme of their music remained focused on love and peace.

Father Knows Best was a family sitcom about a middle-class family, the Andersons, and starred the easy-going Robert Young, Jane Wyatt, his charming wife, and their children. The likeable Young always seemed to have the right answer to resolve various Anderson family concerns.

Many TV westerns were the rage in the 1950s. The TV *Gunsmoke* series, which was centred in and around Dodge City, starred handsome James Arness as the upright Marshal Matt Dillon. With a run of twenty-two years, it was the most popular of all TV westerns.

The Perry Como Show was another popular TV program with my family. Como was a successful American singer and TV personality, whose theme song was "Dream Along with Me."

Hockey Night in Canada started in 1952 and remains a national institution that is still going strong. When the Toronto Maple Leaf games was first televised, Foster Hewitt was the commentator and coined the phrase "He shoots, he scores!" Danny Gallivan was another key TV hockey personality, mainly covering the Montreal Canadian games. He also coined some humorous phrases, like "nowhere near the net" when a shot would go wide, and "cannonading shot" and "spinnerama" moves. Both Hewitt and Gallivan were popular and highly respected hockey commentators. At the time, there were only six teams in the original National Hockey League: Boston, Detroit, Chicago, Montreal, New York, and Toronto. Many fans knew the names of almost all of the players and the coaches. Without fail, my mother would grill some hamburgers for me for dinner on Saturday night, which I'd eat with a bag of salted Old Dutch potato chips while I watched *Zorro*, which, at the time, aired just before *Hockey Night in Canada*. *Zorro* was a Walt Disney production that premiered in 1957 and featured a masked swordsman who duelled with an assortment of villains in nineteenth century Spanish California.

Don Messer's Jubilee was another highly-rated Canadian television program, broadcast nationwide by CBC out of Halifax, Nova Scotia, from 1957 until 1969. It starred Don Messer, Charlie Chamberlain, and Marg Osburne. By the mid-1960s, it earned higher ratings than *The Ed Sullivan Show.*

Front Page Challenge was also a very popular Canadian television quiz show that required panelists to identify a mystery challenger, who was usually an important figure in a major Canadian news story. The program began in 1957. The regular panelists for many years were the often loud and often outspoken former globe-trotting journalist Gordon Sinclair, journalist and television personality Betty Kennedy, and scholarly best-selling author Pierre Berton, along with respected and always dignified moderator Fred Davis.

We also watched the popular *Wayne & Shuster Show* that featured the Canadian comedy duo Johnny Wayne and Frank Shuster. These renowned comedians were also frequent guests on *The Ed Sullivan Show.* They had one of the most popular runs of all comedians in North America.

SUMMERTIME IN THE PASS

Family vacations were uncommon. I can only remember a couple of them, one to Kalispell, Montana, and another to Baines Lake, British Columbia. We did, however, have some vacations with relatives in Calgary and Lethbridge that were a real treat. Most of my friends went nowhere. Highlights of these visits were times spent at the Lethbridge Exhibition and Rodeo and Calgary Stampede. We usually took a Greyhound bus to Calgary with a stopover and transfer at a depot in Fort McLeod, which featured a restaurant. I'd savour these trips because my mother would usually let me buy a hamburger and milkshake. There was also the odd family camping trip beside the Oldman River, north of Cowley. Notably, Greyhound cancelled services in western Canada in 2018.

Ted Amos with a couple of fine trout, 1968 (Photo Credit: Dennis Amos).

Ted Amos often took me along on camping and fishing trips to local trout streams throughout the Oldman River drainage with his son Dennis. I'd just walk a short distance from home to fish in the Crowsnest River. On trips with Ted, Dennis and I would turn over "cow pies" (i.e., the dung of cattle) with sticks in our search for maggots to use as bait, or we'd beat the grass to catch grasshoppers. Ted would usually catch some aquatic bugs that locals used to call "devil scratchers" (i.e., larval stoneflies) and hellgrammites (i.e., larval mayflies) from the creeks using a homemade framed screen. Just about everybody also had a jar of Golden Nugget salmon eggs, a favourite bait particularly for trout.

Although vacations were rare there were festive community events to celebrate. The Victoria Day long weekend in May and also July 1, in particular, featured picnics and races for the kids, and pop and candy were free for children. There was an annual fair and rodeo with rides in the grounds in Coleman and Blairmore, which were popular attractions. However, most kids learned to play outside during all seasons; there were no video games or the like, and few kids were glued to TV sets or the radio.

One of my chores was the daily grocery run for my mom during the summertime. Each day, I would run errands for her and pick up the mail. Usually, Dennis Amos, who was one of my best friends and still is, and I would head out together so that he could also do some chores for his mother. We always made a point of stopping in to visit my aunt Beatrice in the Johnson and Cousins Dry Goods store on Main Street in Bellevue. Aunt Beatie was a clerk in the store and had a soft spot for us youngsters. Not a day went by during the summer that we didn't drop by and ask for some money for some candy. A nickel or dime would do the trick. Many years later, Dennis would come up to my aunt Beatie and ask her, "You got anything in your 'poise,' Aunt Beatie?" How could she not give us kids something, eh?

My aunt Beatrice (Beatie) moved to Calgary where she married Albert Christie. My uncle Fred Radford was the only relative on the Radford side of the family who remained in the Pass with his wife, Margaret, where he operated Radford Insurance Agency in Blairmore. Their family consisted of sons Gordon and Donald and daughter, Joan. He later sold his business, which was renamed Crowsnest Insurance Agencies Ltd. Fred also served as a local magistrate where he developed a reputation as a fair but tough judge with local RCMP and Alberta Fish and Wildlife Division game wardens. They affectionately nicknamed him "Black Fred" for his stern justice to law breakers. He told me one story of some minors in Bellevue who appeared before him on an illegal liquor possession charge. When he asked who supplied the illegal booze, they said they found it in an alley. He said that was hard to believe and the second time he'd heard this story during that particular court session. He couldn't believe anybody would be so stupid as to leave beer lying around in a back alley. Needless to say, they were charged by Uncle Fred.

On the way to Main Street, we would have to pass by some residences where dog fights were always a danger. Dennis's dog, Bingo, who was part Airedale, used to have some dandy scraps with a neighbourhood dog named Chipper, a mongrel with a lot of collie in him and owned by the Ellison family. Chipper had a thick pelt and a hide like a buffalo. Bingo would tag along whenever Dennis and I went on errands. We had to pass by the Ellison house where Chipper lived on the way uptown.

As we approached this house, we were always on full alert. Bingo's hair would stand on end, his tail would be held high, and a menacing growl would come from deep within his throat. Chipper would often be lying in wait and would spring from his favourite hiding place beside a fence. The dog fight was on! Dog hair would fly; yelps would get the attention of the neighbours. There was nobody brave enough to step in and try to break up the fights, so out would come the garden hoses to cool the dogs off. After a thorough soaking, the fight would end just as quickly as it had started. It wasn't uncommon for hides to be torn. Dennis and I would continue our journey. This scene was repeated time and time again for many years until Bingo and Chipper reached their old age, when they grudgingly just circled each other, legs held high, peeing as they went.

NEIGHBOURS—THE AMOS AND FARFUS FAMILIES AND OTHERS

To the west, our next-door neighbours were Albert Edward "Ted" and Sylvia "Sally" Amos and their children, Beverley (Joan), Elaine, Allan (Chuck), and Dennis. Ted passed away in 1982 and Sally in 2005.

Dennis, one of my best friends, was a star hockey player back in the day. He played on teams above his age level. His nickname became the "Famous Amos"; he was that good. He had a cannonading shot like Bobby Hull. It would make any player duck.

Ted was a coal miner, who worked in various underground mines, the last one being the tunnel mine at Vicary Creek, north of Coleman. Ted and Sally had one of the best gardens in town. Gardens were important because fresh vegetables could often be hard to find and were also expensive. Ted always seemed to be chewing gum. Whenever I visited him, he'd invariably ask me to give him my best punch in his gut as a test of my strength. Usually, no matter how hard I hit him, he didn't wince until I got in my teens, when he said I had developed quite a wallop. Ted was like a second father to me, and I have many fond memories of him. He'd take me and Dennis to most of our out-of-town hockey games, as far off as in Fernie, British Columbia. I don't ever remember him missing our home games, where he and Huberte Mattson were regulars. Very few parents went to their kid's hockey games, so the players always appreciated their support. Hockey was the only organized sport during the time I grew up in the Pass.

Elaine, Dennis, Joan, and Allan (Chuck) Amos (L–R);
Radford house to the right (Photo Credit: Dennis Amos).

I'd often go on camping trips with Ted and his family, in his family sedan, quite often to Dutch Creek. Many residents of the Pass were keen outdoorsmen and women. People enjoyed camping, and it was a major source of recreation at the time. In addition to the adventures of camping, we'd go fishing for cutthroat trout in

Dutch Creek. This was long before the days of holiday trailers and recreational vehicles. We'd sleep in canvas tents and hope it didn't rain because they weren't waterproof. Often meals would be made over a campfire or on a Coleman stove fuelled with white gas. At the time, there was a locked gate on an old logging road beside the creek. Vehicle traffic was prohibited during the fire season. We'd walk up the road for a few miles and then fish our way downstream back to the campsite.

Back then there was no such thing as catch and release fishing. We caught fish to eat them. Just about every angler had a wicker creel to keep their catch. During the summer, we'd line the creel with fresh grass and pack the grass around any trout or "grayling" (Rocky Mountain whitefish) we caught. When we stopped to fish a pool, we'd put the creel in the cool water. That way the fish stayed fresh until we went home or returned to camp. We'd clean the fish at the end of the day. If we were going home, we'd always save the fish heads for family cats, which went crazy over them. I don't know what it is about fish heads, but it brings out the animal side in a household cat.

The Forestry Trunk Road, northward from Coleman through the Kananaskis country to Hinton and Edson, was completed in 1951. Ted would take this dusty gravel road, in the Crowsnest Forest Reserve, up and over the Vicary Creek summit to get to Dutch Creek. It was not uncommon for most period cars to boil over by the time they reached the summit, so you'd have to pull over to the side of the road until the radiator cooled down and top it up with water before resuming your trip.

A gateway marked the entrance to the forest reserve, where it was a requirement to complete a registration form. By law, each party had to complete a registration form with their name and address, purpose of the trip, date, and, if hunting, list the make and calibre of any firearms. You were supposed to drop off your portion of the registration form when you left the forest reserve. I could never understand the purpose of this registration process, as it seemed archaic and daft. However, most people complied with this registration process, which could be a pain during the hunting season, in particular, as it would be dark when vehicles arrived at the gate and lineups weren't unusual. There'd almost always be a scramble trying to fill in the form in the dark. It wasn't uncommon for some people to throw away the pencils used to fill out the registration form to delay hunters back in the queue so they could get a head start on prime hunting spots.

In 1952, the year I started Grade 1, Kazimierz (Kaz) Farfus and his wife, Maria, settled into life in Bellevue, in a house just to the east of our place. Kaz was born in Zawoda, Poland; Maria in Sitaniec, Poland. He met Maria in Germany, and they were married in 1949. Together with their families, Kaz and Maria immigrated to Canada in 1950, where they had a contract to work on a sugar beet farm in the Lethbridge area. Two years later, they moved to Bellevue, where they established a permanent home next door to ours and raised their three sons: Walter, George, and Richard. Kaz worked at the Burmis Sawmill and several mines throughout the Crowsnest Pass area, including the Bellevue Underground Mine. Kaz seemed most at home in his garden—one of the largest in our neighbourhood—digging in the soil, planting, watering, and tending to his vegetables. Kaz and Maria were good neighbours. They were simple and loving people who often came to house parties at our home. Maria passed away in 2016 and Kaz in 2017.

Harry and E. R. (Clemence) Jepson lived on the block just to the north of our house, with their children, James (Jim) and Helene. Jim was always a top student. A trail blazer, Clemence Jepson, better known as "Clem," was the first woman mayor to take office in the Crowsnest Pass in 1963 after serving on council for three years. Harry used to go on fishing trips with Ted Amos, Dennis, and I. Harry was a keen angler, who was always amazed at how successful Dennis and I often were, especially when we reeled in some large trout. I chalked this up mainly to beginner's luck; however, even as kids, we were also keen, skilled anglers.

Dick Koentges, who had a trucking business, lived in the house to the east of the Warren House, where big rigs were often parked beside the residence. Dick married Kathy McDonald, a vivacious woman from Blairmore that I used to date in my teens.

There was an abandoned house with a detached garage owned by a mysterious Colonel Warren, next to the Koentges' house. Colonel Warren's house was a "ghost house," whose owners never resided in it and left it fully furnished with some odd souvenirs, the most peculiar one being a stuffed alligator. The house was fully furnished, appearing as though the owners simply walked away never to return, as though it was caught up in a time warp. None of my friends knew anything about Colonel Warren or his wife or family. When I was young, all the doors and windows were locked with the drapes closed. Over time, some vandals broke into the house, started to ransack it, and likely stole whatever was of value. Nobody seemed to know anything about the Warren family. There was a rumour Colonel Warren was a veteran of the Boer War.

Jim and Zena Svoboda, with their children, Sharon, Jim (Sibby), Larry, Marilyn, Linda, and Lori, lived in a house overlooking the Bellevue Mine. Jim (senior) was an ardent and very successful big game hunter and an exceptionally good angler. He had a smoke house at the back of his yard, where he'd smoke trout and "grayling" (Rocky Mountain whitefish) as well as bear meat, on occasion. He'd soak the fish in a brine solution overnight before smoking them. They were the tastiest fish I've ever eaten. Jim was also a celebrity for his famous pickled eggs, which he sold to the Bellevue Legion.

The names of the families who lived on the street to the north of us (from west to east) were Basso, Hunger, Jepson, Koentges, Warren, Hovan, Svoboda, and Krywalt.

We had some interesting neighbours who lived on the Flats to the east of our house. The Joe Gramacci family was of Italian descent;

Joe raised goats in his backyard (to eat), which sometimes used to perch on top of his buildings. Bill McInnis, of Scottish origin, whose family came from Cape Breton Island, would sometimes get dressed up in tartans with a kilt; he'd march along the road in front of our house, playing his bag pipes, I presume, to commemorate some Scottish milestones. Bill was known to imbibe heavily and often got royally drunk, and I mean "royally" inebriated.

CHILDHOOD VISITS AT PAPA AND GRANDMA SAPETA'S HOME

I was lucky because I had grandparents in the Pass; not all of my friends were so fortunate. If my parents took a holiday, they'd drop off my brother and I at our grandparent's house in Coleman. Grandma was as patient as a saint with us, whom she affectionately called "boyses" until the day I hit Jimmy on the side of his head with one of Papa's broken bowling pins I found in the pantry. The splintered bowling pins were used as firewood. This was long before recycling became popular. Papa was just being frugal; nothing went to waste. A few old pins were lying beside the coal stove in the kitchen, and I knocked my brother out cold. Grandma wailed that I had killed Jimmy, but he eventually came around. How she put up with us is anybody's guess, but after that visit, Grandma asked my mom to bring only one boy at a time, saying, "Carrie, they're just too much for me to handle when they're together. They're nice boys, but I can only handle one at a time from now on."

Granny had somehow learned how to be a ventriloquist, and after every bedtime story, never fail, there would be voices from elsewhere in the house. "The boogeyman," she used to say. "Go to sleep or the boogeyman will get you." That was enough warning for me. I never made so much as a peep afterwards and buried my head under the quilt.

Jim (L) and Duane Radford at Bellevue home (circa 1955).

One summer, when I was visiting by myself, I fell out of a large poplar tree in her front yard and knocked myself unconscious. She found me lying under the tree and carried me into the house before beckoning the local doctor. In those days, doctors still made house calls, and he pronounced that I would live but to stay out of trees forever. Poor Granny was worried sick and thought that she was on the verge of losing me—small wonder.

Another time a neighbour's dog attacked me as I walked into her yard. The little mongrel bit me on my mouth and I needed over a dozen stitches. What a fright! The doctor patched me up and said that I would never grow a good mustache. He was right, as hair won't grow on the scar tissue. "Never bend down to pet a dog," Granny always said, "because they might bite you." I guess I should have listened to her warning. What I experienced was a normal part of growing up in the Pass—just about every kid had some kind of misadventure.

Duane with a Belgian hare at Papa Sapeta's home in Coleman (circa 1952).

Speaking of being bitten, my brother, Jimmy, had a nasty encounter with one of my grandfather's Belgian hares. Papa liked the taste of rabbits and raised the large-bodied Belgian hares for table fare. He had a few rabbit pens in his backyard, which held hares. One fine Sunday, he decided it was time to slaughter one of the old bucks and asked me and Jimmy to help him. We used to delight in holding the big hares by their ears when it was necessary to take them out of their pens, usually to clean the pens. This was no small job for a boy because the hares probably weighed between six to nine pounds and some of the largest must have topped ten pounds. On this occasion, it was time to dispatch one of the old fellows. It was a sad day for us boys because the hares were quite tame and we treated them as pets. But, in those days people regularly raised animals for food and had to kill them for the table. Anyway, Jimmy was going to do the job today under Papa's supervision.

Papa told Jimmy to hold the hare by its ears and give it a sharp blow to the back of its head with a club. I know this sounds simple enough, but it was all that Jimmy could do to hold the large hare with one hand and swing the club with his free hand. He lost his grip on the rabbit's ears and it started to slip. He dropped the club and grabbed the hare by its back feet so that it wouldn't fall. As soon as he had hold of its feet, the hare swung around and bit him hard on his finger. Blood spurted. That's why you hold a rabbit by its ears so it can't bite you! It was quite a commotion before Papa managed to grab hold of the big hare and free Jimmy from its bite. Grandpa had enough of the hare's shenanigans and, without further adieu, quickly clubbed the hare to death. Jimmy had stopped squealing by then, and it was off to bandage his finger. This was all in a day's routine, and nobody said anything about the incident, which wasn't considered unusual. Lots of locals raised rabbits in pens as a source of fresh meat as well as chickens.

Sandra Newton (cousin), unknown girl, Jim and Duane Radford (L–R) at Sapeta home in Coleman (circa 1952)—note the two-seater toilet in background.

On hot summer days, Granny would set up a galvanized wash basin outside and fill it with pails of water from her well, which was inside the porch at the time. The well had a hand pump from which cold, clear water would gush. Two small kids could fit inside the tub at the same time, although it was a tight squeeze. Such were the things we did to amuse ourselves. Life was simple, and kids did not have high expectations for fun and entertainment. There were no video or computer games or apps, and so on—you had to make your own fun.

ATTENDING ELEMENTARY SCHOOL— CRUEL AND UNUSUAL PUNISHMENT?

I took my elementary grades at the Bellevue Elementary School, which was originally a four-room school, that opened in 1912 and closed in 1960. The school was enlarged in 1919 to include additional classrooms and offices. It was located just north of Highway 3.

During my school years, Highway 3 ran smack through the middle of Bellevue when I was an elementary student. There was a sharp turn on the highway just west of the school that was notorious for vehicle rollovers, especially semi-trailer trucks. I can also remember seeing several lumber trucks that rolled over and lost their loads, freight trucks carrying produce that broke open and spilled produce all over the ditch, and lots of cars that rolled over. Once, Kenny Noble was riding his horse and got hit by a coal truck on the highway corner between Victor's Barber Shop and the Bellevue Elementary School. Kenny got his leg busted up, and his horse was killed.

As was the custom of the day, the girls and boys formed separate lines before marching into school at the start of the day. During the winter, recess would be in the school basement, where kids did their usual thing, running around, with boys teasing girls, some boys bullying other kids, and children playing table tennis (or ping pong) to burn off energy. If the weather was warm, everyone went outside for recess in the school yard, where there were swings and teeter-totters. Mr. Cox used to be a fixture in the Bellevue school; he was the school caretaker and kept the furnaces going in the winter time. Kids would watch him sitting in his room in the basement and eating his lunch during their lunch break.

According to archival records in the Glenbow Museum in Calgary, Mrs. Jean Shafer (nee Fisher) was my Grade 1 teacher. One of my old classmates remembered her as a wonderful, understanding, kind, and considerate teacher. My recollections of her are not as fond.

The aforementioned archival records were a Department of Education Daily Register for Recording the Attendance of Pupils in the Bellevue-Hillcrest S.D. No. 1336 for the school year 1952–1953. Similar records were available for 1953–1954, 1954–1955, and 1955–1956. Interestingly, the school was closed during the first and second week of September that year "due to polio," which was a dreaded childhood disease.

Dorothy Vowk (please note that her name is sometimes erroneously spelled "Volk") was my Grade 2 teacher in 1953–1954, when I came down with the measles during the first week of November and was attended to by Dr. D. S. White on November 8. Mrs. Shafer taught me in Grade 3 and 4 in 1954–1955 and 1955–1956. It was interesting that she recorded in the "Notes on absences" that children missed school due to rheumatic fever, mumps, "operation on eye," and chicken pox.

During 1955–1956, Mary Kerr was a long-serving substitute teacher as well as Juane Mattson. Some other school teachers in the Bellevue Elementary School while I was in elementary school were Isabel Dambois, Mr. M. D. McEachern (principal), Alice Serra, Mrs. M. Urbash, and Mrs. M. Utley.

Mrs. Dambois was my teacher in Grades 5 and 6 and was one of the finest teachers I ever had. Interesting, prior to my going to elementary school, my second cousin Anne Sapeta (1952) and my aunt Beth Shevels also taught there.

Duane Radford, circa 1956.

The Cold War (1947–1991) had created a specter of fear throughout the world by the time I began Grade 1. I'm sure that every kid in Canada was frightened that there might be a nuclear war with Russia and that if atomic bombs didn't kill you outright, then nuclear fallout would. Bellevue had a siren that was to sound in the event of an attack. Children were drilled on how to seek shelter from a bomb blast both in school and at home. We'd been told to kneel under our school desks and take shelter in our basements at home in the event a bomb was dropped, a possibility because of all the coal mines. Nobody had a bomb shelter, per se, in Bellevue, which just added to the fear factor because there were newspaper stories of rich families in some Canadian cities that had them. I recall the frightening sound of the siren, which terrified children. I can also still vividly remember reading *On the Beach* by Nevil Shute, a 1957 post-apocalyptic novel about the final days of the civilized world following a global nuclear war, where civilization in the northern hemisphere was annihilated.

Canadians had one of their first exposures to world terrorism with the Mau Mau Uprising (1952–64), also known as the Mau Mau Rebellion, where several tribal peoples fought against the white European colonist-settlers in Kenya, the British army, and the local Kenya regiment; it was a portent to widespread terrorism in the following decades.

One of the earliest major highlights in our elementary school was the coronation of Queen Elizabeth on June 2, 1953, which was celebrated throughout Canada. Local school kids received a commemorative mug to mark the occasion.

While there was no AIDS at the time, instead there were the worrisome childhood diseases characteristic of the 1950s, which were a real concern: cancer, polio, whooping cough, and tuberculosis. Penicillin was the only antibiotic I recall. I did have a close health call, however, and ended up in an isolation room for several days in the Crowsnest Pass Hospital when I was still a child from what I presume was a virus. It was scary. No visitors were allowed. I was in isolation under quarantine until I eventually got better.

The polio epidemic in the early 1950s crippled tens of thousands of Canadians until the Salk vaccine was introduced in 1955. This deadly disease was another major worry in all families. While growing up, there was a classmate who had been infected by the polio virus and she was relegated to a wheel chair for the rest of her life. Also, I remember when the Salk vaccine became available, my mother marched me down to the local high school to get the vaccine. The fear of polio in those days was very real and every bit as frightening as the COVID-19 pandemic in 2020–2022. The anti-vaxxers of today were unheard of; nobody I knew shied away from getting vaccinated.

Fistfights were uncommon during my elementary school years but not unheard off. They usually took place after school or on weekends, off the school grounds. They were talked up during classes, so there was generally a crowd of students when the kids squared off. Teachers would break up fights that took place at school. I was only involved in a few fistfights, which typically didn't last very long. The secret was to get in the first good punch or two. That was usually enough to win. It boiled down to good timing. I discovered, there are no winners in fistfights. I still bear the marks of a dislocated knuckle and broken finger on my right hand, reminders of former street fights.

Some of the fights were personal between rivals from different towns to see who was toughest. Most fights usually didn't go more than a few rounds because they were so tiring. They were usually settled with a bloody nose or jab to the jaw, which knocked the opponent to the ground, putting an end to the fight. It was the custom for fighters to shake hands after the fight as a show of faith, that there were no hard feelings. Sometimes, however, the looser would muster some brothers or friends to engage in another fight to settle the score. I don't believe in fistfights to resolve differences but admit that you had to learn to stand up for yourself, especially in the Pass, or you'd be bullied by other kids, some of whom were mean and could be cruel.

There were frequent incidents of corporal punishment with a strap or spankings while I attended elementary school, and some in junior high school. I received a strapping on more than one occasion. Although the strap has generally been out of use in Canada since around the 1970s, corporal punishment in schools was in accordance with federal law until January 30, 2004, when it became outlawed under Section 43 of the Criminal Code. A leather strap would be very intimidating, at least a foot long, about two inches wide and a quarter-inch thick. Strapping was an accepted form of discipline to correct what a teacher deemed unacceptable behaviour often for no really good reason. It is a sad legacy, however, and some of my former classmates remain mentally scared by what happened to them.

Some were given the strap for simply getting the wrong answer to a question too often, which doesn't justify such punishment. A friend of mine was so afraid of one teacher, he'd often vomit each morning before leaving for school. Once, after being spanked with a wooden slat, he defecated in his pants, he was so scared of this teacher. It wasn't uncommon for teachers to strap students in front of the whole class, which was absolutely humiliating. Usually, the child would be asked to turn one of their hands up and the teacher would come down hard on the palm of their hand, often more than once. Some teachers preferred to strap children on their wrist. Other's gave the strap on the buttocks. Some refused to strap children. It was a rare kid who did not cry after being strapped.

Later, by the time I reached Grade 8, only principals gave the strap, in private, in their office. From what I've been told, they usually didn't stop until a student broke into tears. Some teachers, however, also used mind games to frighten other students; they forewarned those kids who were going to get a strapping, which would be at the end of the day's classes. Corporal punishment would be in the back of their minds all day until the time of reckoning arrived. Most children did their best to be brave and not cry, but few succeeded. I got my first strapping in Grade 1 for alleged behavioural issues, which, to this day, I do not feel was warranted.

Some teachers could be very rough. On one occasion, a teacher grabbed a fellow student by the ears and threw him into the cloakroom. It wasn't unusual to get bonked with a teacher's wooden pointer for what they considered bad behaviour. Most of the time, a student would be banished to the corner of a room for some quiet time if they stepped out of line. Further, it was common for students to be kept after school to "write lines" as punishment and to try change their behaviour. Chewing gum in class was forbidden. Some teachers would make children put the wad of gum on their noses as punishment, where it would remain for some time to deter other kids. Most kids would take gum out of their mouths at the sign of trouble and stick it on the bottom of their desks.

I contacted some of my former classmates while researching this book. Almost all of them had trouble sorting out their elementary teachers. I can't help but wonder if this might be a result of some sort of self-defence mechanism or symptom of a post-traumatic stress disorder. There were also stories about parents taking their trauma- tized kids to the local doctor in Bellevue, who said he been visited by other parents whose children had experienced similar trauma symptoms after being strapped or disciplined.

I didn't consider myself a bad kid or a troublemaker. I did, however, have a habit of being a bit of tease and could be a bit rambunctious at times. I guess I could have been called a prankster. When I was a child, however, I thought that I was generally well behaved. I did not go around picking fights but did not back down when intimidated. This would be seen as a sign of weakness and lead to more bullying. You had to learn to stand up for yourself; if not, you'd be harassed by mean kids of which there were several, notably from one family from Blairmore and two families from Hillcrest.

With discipline, in the form of corporal punishment, unequivo- cally swift at schools in the Crowsnest Pass, I was to learn some lessons the hard way in the Bellevue Elementary School. Actually, I didn't get off to a good start. My mother was under doctor's orders to stay home when the time came for me to register in Grade 1 at the Bellevue school. She was still convalescing from the birth of my sister, Jill, on August 7, 1952. We didn't find out until my mother had a heart attack later in life that she only had one kidney, which may have contributed to complications after my sister was born. She suffered from debilitating kidney stones a few years afterwards and had to be hospitalized in Calgary for treatment.

My aunt Alice Williams got the job of walking me to school on my first day. I didn't stay there long, and by recess, I was back at home. I just didn't like Grade 1. My mother was consternated and kept asking me why I had come home. "Well, Mom, I just don't like school. I'd rather stay home with you," I pleaded, to no avail, and before long Aunt Alice had me back in class.

In the 1950s, teachers had a lot of clout. If you got in trouble at school, it could be even worse at home. If I misbehaved, there were the interminable lines that I would have to stay after school and write. For example, write fifty lines of "I will be quiet in class" or something like that. There was no sense trying to fool my mother. When I was late, there were questions to be answered. My biggest fear was that I might fail, a threat often used by certain teachers, which would be a disgrace to my family. I didn't know what would be worse: having to face my parents with the bad news or having to put up with another year under them. There was the odd teacher who said I probably wouldn't amount to much and would never make it to university. I think they were the source of my apprehension about going to university. Alberta's universities always seemed so foreign and far away to a young boy in a small town, being hundreds of miles from the nearest one. But, in their own perverted way, they also served up a challenge, and I became determined to prove them wrong.

I thought that one of my teachers, Dorothy Vowk, was an angel. This is where I learned about positive motivation. Punishment will make children wary but will not necessarily change their behaviour. Rewards will make them become better behaved, as there is something positive to be gained. Ms. Vowk helped turn me into a better student with her positive influence and small rewards, such as pencils and crayons, which she paid for out of her own pocket to motivate students. While I recall getting the strap at least once in elementary school, I didn't get the strap again until Grade 7, along with a couple of my friends, for what I still think was a petty reason. I definitely do not believe in corporal punishment because teachers should not be judge and jury, and for other good reasons.

Not that I didn't come close to getting the strap on another occasion in Grade 3 if my memory is correct. I broke out in hysterical laughter when one of my classmates accidentally dropped their crayons. How could I know that Mr. McEachern, the principal, was at the door, right behind me? Without so much as a peep, he swooped down and grabbed me by the scruff of my neck, carrying me like a little mouse back to his office. I have never been so scared in my life.

The principal was absolutely dreaded by all the students for his scowl and fierce look. Nobody, but nobody, crossed him! Fortunately, my school record was pretty clear, thank goodness. Otherwise, I'm sure I would have been expelled. After a stern lecture about my inappropriate behaviour, I was solemnly marched back to the class, as an example for all. He was a wise old man, though, because he made me sit tight in his office for a good half an hour while he said he was going to consult with my teacher to see whether I still had a place in the Bellevue Elementary School. I hardly breathed until he returned. He poured over my records, which weren't much from what I recall, before finally passing judgment. I was learning that elementary school was all business. I should have known better, what with the segregation of the boys and the girls and the lineup before marching into school before classes began. The place was run like an army boot camp!

For a while, I was the class hero when I showed up at school one morning with half a pound of blood-soaked gauze taped around my right ear. I'd had a stroke of bad luck the night before, during a boy's sword fight in the undeveloped property beside the school grounds.

This was our play on Black Beard and Robin Hood stories, I guess. Practically every night, my friends and I would play "crusaders" in this area using some surveyor's stakes (or laths) that we stole from a local lumberyard as make-believe swords. This was always great fun and gave us many hours of enjoyment.

Unfortunately, on this particular evening, in the heat of the battle, my opponent had me backing up with an aggressive frontal attack. It was my misfortune to back right into a rusty old barbed wire fence, which promptly almost cut off my right ear. There was blood all over. My friends thought they had seen the last of me. As luck would have it, I was very close to Dr. Milton's practice and residence, the local doctor at the time. My friends escorted me to his home where he had an office. Dr. Milton was aghast when he opened the door. I think he thought I was done for, what with blood all over my head. Undaunted, he directed me into his office, which was well equipped, all things considered. Then the stitches began: all seventeen of them to re-attach my ear to my head. This was too much for one of my friends, who passed out and slid under the operating table. "Enough is enough. One patient is all I can handle at a time," Dr. Milton said, telling another boy to get rid of my friend and drag him into the waiting room.

The next morning, about ten kids arrived at my house to walk to school with me. They all wanted to see my ear. I'm not sure if they thought I wouldn't make it through the night. For some time thereafter, I was the class hero. The teacher fawned over me out of sympathy for my plight. I think my classmates might have figured I was almost a goner. I had their undivided sympathies. My mom put an end to the sword fighting from that day forward. How she put up with me on occasions like this is beyond me. But, like all mothers, she remembers only that I was a good boy when I was growing up.

During elementary school, I learned to keep my nose clean and stay out of trouble. These were uneventful years, except for my dreaded piano lessons, which my mother insisted I take when I was in Grade 1. The piano lessons would continue for several more years until the best teacher I had, Bellevue's Hazel McDonald, met an untimely death. I usually detested practising the piano. However, there was no bike riding or playing with friends until I had put in my daily half hour at least.

I had developed into a pretty good scraper by Grade 5 and 6. My dad's business partner, Johnny Raymaker, had given him a pair of boxing gloves by this time. "If you boys are going to fight all the time, you may as well have some boxing gloves and do it right," Dad used to say. I didn't really like the boxing gloves, which were quite big, so you couldn't really deliver a knockout punch with them. We had interminable boxing matches. I'm not sure how many I won. In the process, I developed a bit of a reputation with some of the neighbours who wanted their sons to be able to defend themselves. One of the fathers would pay me a dime to scrap with his son, to hone his self-defence skills; I guess I was his sparring partner. The boy and I were good friends and got along well. Unfortunately, he had a soft nose, which would bleed easily. The staged fights rarely lasted very long. I didn't like to earn my spending money this way but was too naïve to say no—how could I help not oblige his dad?

Then there were Saturday night "tag-team" matches that Jimmy and I had with the Amos brothers, Dennis and Allan (Chuck). Wrestling was the in thing, and all the kids watched it on television. A Canadian professional wrestler best known by his ring name "Whipper" Billy Watson was one of our heroes. The Midget Wrestling Warriors were a close second. So, after my parents left for a night on the town, we would invite the Amos brothers over for a tag-team match. My sister, Jill, would be scolded not to mention anything to Mom and Pa, and sworn to secrecy or put to bed before the matches began. Then we boys would clear all the furniture from the middle of the living room, and the tag-team match would begin. We would wrestle until we were exhausted. Like my aunt Helen used to say, "Monkey see, monkey do!"

KIDS' GAMES

Back in the day, kids had to make the most of whatever came their way by way of amusement in the Pass. There were no video games, few organized sports, television was in its infancy, and local reception was poor. Organized sports were practically unheard of, save for what went for a minor hockey program, which usually fell apart. There were no organized soccer games, softball or baseball games, swimming lessons, or anything of the sort.

I learned how to swim in a gravel pit near the Frank Slide that had filled with ground water and runoff. I can still remember how cool the water felt on a hot summer's day. In my early teens, I'd hitchhike to the hamlet of Burmis, about five miles east of Bellevue, in the foothills, to swim in the weedy, spring-fed Burmis Lake. What a treat it was to eat saskatoon berries and wild strawberries on the hills surrounding the lake, and to drink from the cool spring that fed it all summer long.

When I got a bit older, I graduated to Lees Lake, which was a good ten miles from town and a long way to hitchhike for young kids. I was terrified of the "weeds" (i.e., aquatic vegetation) in Lees Lake. We had all heard tales of weeds grabbing unsuspecting swimmers and dragging them to their death. "They'll pull you down," kids used to say, and I'm sure that no one bothered to question this saying.

When I got older and discovered girls, I would hitchhike to Frank, where the one-and-only outdoor swimming pool in the Pass was located, at the Turtle Mountain Motel beside the Crowsnest River, which has long since been demolished. The chlorine in the footbath was enough to take the hide off your feet. But what fun it was to swim in clean water where you could actually see the bottom. You didn't have to even worry about garter snakes swimming up beside you while you blissfully swam along in the local ponds. One of these reptiles gave me the fright of my life when it came up right beside my head as I swam across Burmis Lake one fine afternoon. I thought that I was done for!

My friends and I made our own fun and much of it centred around the Bellevue Coal Mine and the Canadian Pacific Railroad tracks, which were on the south side of town. We would push mine carts around for the fun of it and ride our bikes down the immense coal slack piles—motocross before its time. You didn't dare fall or you'd never hear the end of it from your mom when you came home covered in coal dust; not that we didn't fall from time to time, but it was great fun. We'd ride our bikes to the top of the piles along the haul roads and then head for the bottom at top speed, all the while trying to keep our balance and not dig too deep into the coal slack pile; if the front wheel bogged down, you were doomed and your bike would tip over. We would also catch garter snakes and leopard frogs from the local ponds and keep them as pets until our parents found about them and made us let them go.

When we felt adventurous, we would walk along the tracks to the Frank Slide and look for spent railway flares and flashers. The rail gangs used to put flashers on the tracks as a warning of approaching locomotives; flares were put down to warn of parked trains. There were always lost flares beside the tracks that were a real find—they'd burn hot and fast once ignited. The flashers didn't always go off when a train rolled over them, and when we found one, we would explode it by dropping slide rocks on it.

When we heard trains approaching, we'd often put pennies on top of the tracks to have the railcars flatten the copper pennies. After a while, you would develop quite an ear for trains by listening to the hum in the rails. You had to be careful because the railway workers and the Canadian Pacific Railway police had a reputation as a tough lot and would bully kids around. Mom always warned me to watch out for "hobos," those wretched poor men who hitched free rides on the railroad stock. We didn't see them very often, but when we did, we would run as fast as our little feet would carry us back home. When the cars were parked along railway sidings, they were a virtual playground for games of "cops and robbers" or "cowboys and Indians." You could play there all day, hiding in the cars and shooting at your friends—it was like a Hollywood movie set and all for nothing!

Sundays would find us at the Bellevue United Church on Main Street for Sunday school. Some of my friends and I must have been quite a bunch of brats because we were often in trouble with our Sunday school teacher, Mrs. Jerry (Grace) Avoledo. She was a kind-hearted woman, but maybe she expected too much of young kids. For the most part, we were there to have fun, not to learn anything. That was why we went to day school. We would tease the girls, smirk at the teacher, giggle behind her back, forget the lines of the hymns and songs, and get banished to a closet. You really have to wonder how a kid could get into trouble at Sunday school. But we did, to the point where we were permanently banished from attending, no kidding. My mother never understood how you could get kicked out of Sunday school. We were told plainly not to come back until we were ready to behave properly; there was no going back, though.

Our parents did not shelter us kids from taking risks, besides my mother's warning to stay clear of hobos beside the Canadian Pacific Railway tracks near Bellevue. It was not uncommon for a group of young boys to be let loose on their own camping trips for several days, where we'd spend time fishing and shooting gophers. All of my friends had a fishing rod and a .22 calibre rifle. Our parents had some simple gun safety rules: always assume a gun is loaded and never point it at anything you don't intend to shoot; plus make sure of your background and don't shoot at anything on a skyline because bullets could travel over a mile.

We'd collect small pieces of driftwood, which we'd smoke. They had to be perfectly dry, slender with a hole in their pitch. You'd light one end with a match and breath in the smoke at the other end. I can recall a couple of trips like this, where my friends and I camped for what must have been a week or so beside the Oldman River and Racehorse Creek without parental supervision. We'd handle all the camp chores on our own, setting up a tent, gathering firewood, cooking, and keeping the camp clean. We ate a lot of canned goods. Our parents indoctrinated us with their mantra to make sure that the campsite was cleaner when we left than when we arrived. During the day, we'd usually go fishing or shoot gophers. Most of the kids were crack shots and could hit a gopher (actually a ground squirrel) with open sights at twenty-five yards or more.

I remember one time when we were camped beside the Oldman River, Jim Svoboda dropped by to see how we were doing and wet a line in the river. Jim was one of the best anglers I'd ever seen, and it wasn't long before he landed a large rainbow trout for dinner. When I later worked as a regional fisheries biologist for Southern Alberta, stationed in Lethbridge, I'd hire Jim to catch fish for contaminant monitoring purposes. I'd pay him an hourly rate, which was a bargain, as he'd usually catch all the fish that we needed for things such as mercury or pesticide testing in just a few hours, which might have taken me or my staff all day or longer.

EXCURSIONS FROM THE PASS

It wasn't very often that I got out of the Pass on a holiday. My world was my hometown of Bellevue and visits to our relatives in Blairmore and Coleman. Occasionally, we would go to my uncle Walter Sapeta's farm, north of Cowley, for a visit and to get our Christmas turkey or some fresh eggs. These visits were always nothing short of an adventure.

Whenever we arrived, there were turkeys everywhere: in the driveway; on the farm buildings; on top of the cars, tractors and trucks; in the barnyard; beside the house; and even on the roof of the house. There were literally hundreds of them, all gobbling at the same time. It was pretty exciting for a small boy and scary when they swarmed you.

My aunt Stephania Sapeta used to ask Jimmy and I if we would like to collect some of the eggs in the barn. Although she had a chicken coup, the chickens laid eggs all over the farm, especially in the old barn. It was great sport to try to find the eggs. Off we would go with a basket to find them. First, we had to get by all those frightening turkeys. "They won't hurt you, boys. Just walk around them," Auntie would say. I never did like to stare down a turkey, and they would hold their ground until the very end. Only when you rushed them would they move off, with a great outburst of cackles that would scare the pants off of you.

Jimmy and I would save some eggs for the pigpen. My uncle always had a lot of pigs, which he kept in a pen near the barn. "Now you boys stay away from the pigs," he used to say. "They'll eat you alive if you fall in the pen." And he was right; they probably would have. There was a big boar that would gladly eat a little kid without as much as a second thought. With my uncle's warning, for sure we would visit the pigs. Scared stiff, we would hiss at them to get their attention. They would run at us going, "Oink, oink, oink," and stick their noses against the fence, slobbering all over. You could smell them; they were so close. What a stink! They would mill around in the rising dust until they realized it wasn't feeding time, which would come later when they would be slopped after our supper. As they turned around, we would pitch an egg at their rear ends. Then the circus would start as they would chase each other's backside trying to eat the splattered eggs. One time, my uncle happened to come by the pigpen in the middle of all the action. "What's all the commotion about, boys?" he said. "You aren't teasing the pigs, are you?"

"Oh no," we replied. "They're just excited to see us." It used to be great fun until they had licked the eggs off each other and settled down again.

Every so often, we would head to Lethbridge to visit my aunt Helen, my uncle Stuart, and my cousin Sandra. These trips seemed to take forever, even though they were only about two hours long. My brother, Jimmy, and I used to always fight when we were kids. I don't know why, but we just couldn't seem to get along with each other. The trips going to Lethbridge often brought out the worst side of our behaviour. They were even worse coming home, once the excitement of our holiday and the trip to Lethbridge was wearing off. We would start by pushing each other, one thing led to another, and before long, there would be full-scale boxing match going on in the back seat. My mother and dad would warn us to stop and then start yelling at us after a while.

On one memorable trip, my dad said that if we didn't stop, he was going to let me off on the Brocket stretch, a long, fairly straight section of Highway 3 between Fort McLeod and Pincher Station that cut through the Peigan Indian Reserve, as it was called back in the day but now referred to as the Piikani Nation. It didn't have a lot of traffic back in those days. I guess that I was really being bad on this trip; I suppose that I was the prime instigator.

As a child, I'd never had much experience with Indigenous Peoples, but thanks to Hollywood, in my child's mind, I'd seen enough western movies to believe they scalped white men and sometimes kidnapped young kids. I never thought that my dad would actually let me off in the middle of the Indian Reserve. I might never be seen again. But he did. Slowly, he brought the car to a stop. "Out," he said, "I've warned you and you wouldn't listen, so get out!" I thought that he must be kidding. I sat still. No, he started up again. "I said out, and I mean it! Get out or I'll throw you out!"

My mom stood up for me. "I'm sure he'll be good, Sam. Just give him another chance. He's learned his lesson," she pleaded, to no avail.

"Get out, for the final time," he said. I was too scared to cry as I opened the door.

My brother, Jimmy, looked absolutely petrified, but he had been spared. I closed the door and the car drove off, out of sight. I was all by myself, alone on the side of Highway 3 in the middle of an Indian Reserve. I didn't know what to do. There wasn't a car in sight. Remember this was back in the 1950s—at any moment some "Indians" might show up and I would be done for or taken away to their camp. My goose was really cooked now. It was my own fault. I guess I should have listened to Pa, but I didn't think he would let his own son out in "Indian country." I looked to the west; I looked to the east. Nothing was in sight. Only the hot prairie breeze made a sound, whispering as it blew through the short grass prairie. Then I spotted something on the horizon. Whew, it was a car! Maybe I was going to be rescued after all.

As it got closer, I could see that it was our car. Dad was coming back and was going to rescue me after all. I was safe. He drove past me and turned around, bringing the car to a halt. I was ready to be a good boy now. He said to get in the car. Without as much as a word, I climbed into the back seat. He looked me in the eye. "Are you going to behave yourself from now on, Duane?" he asked.

I gulped, and said, "Yes, I won't get in any more fights with Jimmy." You know what? Afterwards, my brother and I got along pretty well and the scraps dropped right off.

3

COAL TOWN KIDS

CHILDHOOD STORIES BY ALLAN (CHUCK) AMOS

My dad bought a two-bedroom house for $240 in Hillcrest. The cost included having it moved from there and set on the foundation in Bellevue. In the home lived my parents, my sisters, Joan and Elaine, and my brother, Dennis, and I. For quite a long time, the whole family slept in one bed. Then my granny Amos had to come and live with us, so three slept at the top of the bed while two slept at the bottom. Later, Dad put an addition on the house, which gave us three bedrooms, the third bedroom being for Joan and Elaine.

We had a coal and wood-burning furnace, which meant keeping the coal bucket full and taking the ashes out. Also, we had no indoor plumbing. Having to go to the outhouse in the winter was not enjoyable. If there was no toilet paper, we used old Eaton's catalogues. Bath time was a real event. Water was heated in a water tank on the side of the coal stove. We bathed in the same water, with some hot water added for the next kid. We sat on the oven door to dry. Later, Dad made a bedroom in the basement for Dennis and I. The girl's old bedroom was turned into a bathroom with sink, toilet, tub, and shower. Having a bathroom was wonderful.

We got a lot of wind in the autumn, some of which was hurricane force. I remember one time; I was coming back from Coleman with Sam and Jim Radford. Sam's old '49 Dodge had a sun visor on it that was almost ripped off by the wind. Afterwards, when we arrived in

Bellevue, we noticed a telephone pole broken in half. As we rounded the corner by the school, we noticed the sign on the drugstore was twisted around. The roof of the shed of the people above us blew between Radford's house and ours and landed in the field across the road. There was a lot of wind damage that day!

SNOW! Boy did we get snow, and a lot of it. The kids didn't mind because we loved playing in it. We would get our outfits wet, change, and get right back out there. We made a toboggan run from the top of the barnyard next door down to the garden gate, about eighty yards. We had a lot of rain too, which, quite often, wadded in over our gumboots.

My dad didn't work every day when things were slow at the mine, so a lot of times, we went without many groceries. We had a big garden in the summer, and Mom made use of everything in it. We also had a root cellar, where we stored waxed veggies, and it kept things somewhat fresh for a long time. I remember there were always salamanders in there. We raised rabbits for food, and Dad went hunting for big game. If my dad got an elk or deer, it would help feed the family for a few months. Having the Crowsnest River just over the hill didn't hurt either; the fish were always biting in the summer.

Lee Sickoff, Allan Amos, Wynn Ellison, Dennis Amos, Joy Mole, Jim(my) Radford, and Tommy Woodward (L–R), circa 1950 (Photo Credit: Dennis Amos).

We never got to run up town and buy a bottle of pop, so when Mom made homemade root beer, it was really something. Another thing we ate was dandelion salad. We covered the leaves with a board until they turned yellow and put homemade dressing on them—I didn't mind it at all.

PHOBIAS BY GEORGE DOWSON

I think everyone has had a phobia at one time or another, whether it is snakes, mice, or whatever. Mine was a particular upright vacuum. The year was 1944; I was five years old. My mother, along with a few other ladies, volunteered at the United Church in Bellevue. When it was her turn to clean the church, she took me with her (day care or play school didn't exist). I helped her by stacking the hymn books while she dusted and waxed. When those chores were done, the last thing left was to vacuum the long carpet. This is where I had my first experience with the "Godzilla" of all vacuums. When my mom unlocked the closet door, I couldn't believe my eyes—it was taller than me and menacing-looking, with a long black bag on the back.

Remember, in those days, very few people could afford a vacuum. My mom carefully removed it from the closet, unwound the cord, and plugged it in. I watched as she flipped the toggle switch on the handle. That was when all hell broke loose (at least in my five-year-old mind). That thing wound up like a 747-jet plane; the black bag quickly filled out and snapped to attention, and my eyes got as big as saucers. I just turned around and hauled my butt out of the church as fast as I've ever ran. I didn't even stop to close the door. Once outside, I stopped at the bottom of the church steps and sat down. My mom came rushing out seconds later, trying to assure me that she would not let anything happen to me.

I trusted my mom, but Godzilla the vacuum was a different story. It knew I was afraid of it, and I was sure it would do anything to get me, so I told my mom I would sit on the steps until she was finished. All sorts of thoughts raced through my mind while sitting there listening to the monster whine and roar.

One thought was what if my mom tripped and the vacuum sucked her up. That would just leave my brother, Tom (Butch as some of you knew him by), and me, as my dad was in the army overseas at that time. I really didn't want Tom to be my caregiver, as he often told my mom that he wanted to sell me to the Chinese (Jim's) café for hamburger. I was lucky he was in school the days my mom cleaned the church; otherwise, he would have chased me up and down the streets of Bellevue with that vacuum (but at least he couldn't plug it in). I shuddered at my next thought, as I knew that next Sunday I would have to go back in the church. I devised a plan to go into the church with a bunch of people and I would sit in the middle of the pew. As well, I would look to make sure the lock was on the closet door.

The United Church in Bellevue has been gone for a long time, along with my phobia of Godzilla the upright vacuum. However, I have not, or will not ever buy an upright vacuum.

THE DREADED SPRING CLEAN OUT BY GEORGE DOWSON

It was May of 1950, and I was eleven years old, living in Bellevue. I had just finished a gruelling road hockey season at Raymaker Gardens, ending with Mattson and Stoklosa playing for the Stanley Cup, when I dug out my Alvin Dark Baseball Glove to get ready for the home-and-home series between the Grade 5 and 6 Bellevue Elementary School students and the Grade 5 and 6 at Maple Leaf School students.

But this story is not about hockey or baseball. It's about "the Dreaded Spring Clean Out." Every year, families in the Crowsnest Pass believed they needed to be rejuvenated after a long, hard winter. Whether it was a tonic bought from the Rawley's, or the Watkins man, or a homemade brew, such as sulphur and molasses or molasses and coal oil—all were guaranteed to rejuvenate the body. Every year, my mother would go to Haysom's Bellevue Pharmacy and purchase Beecham's Pills. (Beecham's Pills were a laxative first marketed about 1842 in Wigan, Lancashire.) If she killed us, she could always blame it on the pills.

My brother, Tom, was the first to be rejuvenated, and because he was older, he received a couple more pills than I did. These pills, according to my mother, were designed to rid all the toxins that had accumulated in your body over the winter. COVID-19, and all its variants, would not have had a hope in hell of surviving these cures.

The pills were fairly fast acting: once our stomach started to make rumbling sounds, we stayed as close to the bathroom as possible. The household knew that you had bathroom priority, so there was no sitting and looking through the Eaton's catalogue. Now, if you had outdoor plumbing, and there were quite a few that did, that was a totally different story. First, you'd have to judge the distance from the house to the outhouse, and then your timing had to be perfect. There was no room for error. As well, eating anything before twelve hours was up was useless—as the old saying goes, "in one end, out the other," and in this case was totally true. I'm not quite sure if the pills really did get rid of any toxins, but one thing was for certain that with all that running back and forth to the bathroom and sudden weight loss, we were cleaned out and rejuvenated.

A KID IN BELLEVUE BY DENNIS AMOS

When I started school, I had a very bad teacher—seriously. She used to smash our heads on the desks and pull our ears, pull our hair, take rungs off wooden chairs, and give kids a darn-good, old-fashioned licking. I was sick every day of the week, except Saturday and Sunday. My mom and dad couldn't figure out what was the matter with me! They took me to the local family doctor. The first question he asked my parents was who was my teacher. As things turned out, other parents had complained about this teacher, who ended up getting fired. Because I was so afraid of that teacher, I didn't learn anything that year and had to repeat it, which is how I ended up in class with kids a year younger than me.

Grade 3 and 4, 1955 (Dennis is in the second row to the left, five seats to the back).

We didn't have bathtubs and showers, like we have nowadays, when I was a child. Can you imagine what our moms had to go through washing kids and clothes who played out in the coal fields all the time? I think that my family was one of the last families to get an inside bathroom, a television, and a telephone. The shower was actually the best thing at the time, instead of the Friday-night baths ("bath night" varied among different families) with four of you using the same tub, one after the other.

Then came the television; then the telephone. When we got our first telephone, I couldn't wait to go home and try it out. Once home from school, I went right to the phone, picked it up, and started talking into the receiver. To my surprise, someone started talking back to me. I was so surprised that someone was talking to me without my dialling or anything. (At the time "party lines" were common with many families hooked up to the same line, so eaves-dropping was common. Each phone had a distinctive ring to it.) I hated talking on the phone for a long time after that. To this day, I don't know who that was on the other end of the line. I used to get phone calls from girls when I was in high school. They wouldn't get much of a conversation from me: "Yes . . . No . . . Uh-huh . . . Goodbye"—especially if I thought my mom or dad were listening.

After I got home from school, one of my chores was to shovel coal beside the house into the coal shed room. What I shovelled in an hour, my dad could to in ten minutes. It was also nice when you got a load of briquets because they weren't as dirty as coal and they were easier to light, although they didn't burn as long as a big lump of coal. Then there were the ashes from the coal furnace and stove to take out whenever the ash bins were full. It always seemed like it was windy those days, and you'd end up with ashes in your eyes and hair.

I'll always remember the salamanders we'd invariably find in our cold room in the basement, which was basically just a hole dug into the ground about five feet deep. It had sand on the bottom of the hole to preserve the garden vegetables you put in there for storage over the winter. I always knew that I'd find a salamander or two whenever I went digging for vegetables. How they got there, we never did find out, but they were there all the time we lived in the house.

One day, we were in the Radfords' basement and noticed that there was a big crack in their pantry. Inside the crack, there were three or four mice. We got our cat and thought that we'd put it the pantry and it would catch all the mice. After we threw the cat in the pantry, it bolted and ran away, just like that. It surprised us that the mice chased the cat away! The Radfords had a shower in their basement, which was quite the thing in those days. They also had a real nice big bedroom beside the furnace [Author's Note: The bedroom in the basement was impossible to heat in the winter despite being right beside the coal furnace, and a person could see their breath, it was so cold.]

The Radfords' house had a big deck all the way around its front and side. One day, we were running around the deck and Chucky (my brother) slipped and fell, putting both hands down flat on the deck that was made of rough lumber. You can't imagine how many slivers of wood my mom had to pull out of his hands—maybe fifty or sixty—and there was lots of screaming.

I recall, on another occasion, a fight going on in the Radfords' yard between kids in the neighbourhood when somebody threw a rock that hit Cyril McDonald in the head. Blood spilled everywhere and Cyril yelled that he was calling the cops. Man, I thought that I was going to jail. The cops didn't come, thankfully, because I was terrified of them. We were always having fights with the guys in "River Bottom," a small housing area between Bellevue and Hillcrest, beside the Crowsnest River. Kids would be firing BB guns at each other, throwing fist-sized rocks, and shooting pebbles with sling shots. How nobody ever got blinded or had their teeth knocked out, I don't know. We're all good friends now.

Bingo, the Amos family dog (Photo Credit: Dennis Amos).

The Radfords had a mongrel dog named Nero, and we had a dog named Bingo. The Ellison's had a dog named Chipper. Bingo and Chipper hated each other. If Bingo saw another dog around our place or anywhere else, a dog fight ensued. Bingo used to sleep on the steps at our house. Every day, like clockwork, he would suddenly wake up and take off towards the nearby Catholic Church because he could smell something or hear my dad coming home from work, and he knew he was going to get a leftover sandwich from his lunch pail.

One day, Bingo cut the pad on his foot badly and it bled heavily. We left him at home that day when we went for a walk to our favourite place, Maloff's land, south of the Crowsnest River. When we came home for our five o'clock supper, we found Bingo down by the railroad tracks below our house, but he couldn't stand up or walk. I guess he had tried to follow us to Maloff's but couldn't make it. We went home and got a wagon, loaded him into it, and brought him home. Bob Storey, one of the neighbourhood kids, bandaged him up really good, and in three or four days, he was all better. We never went to a veterinarian in those days because we had no money. (Back in the day, it was rare for any dogs to eat what goes for dog food nowadays; they basically lived off table scraps and whatever else they could find to eat. It was rare for any dog to eat canned or dried dog food.)

Each summer, when we were young kids, we'd put up a big green tent in the Radfords' front yard, beside their garden. I don't think we actually got much sleep because we could hear people walking on the road outside the yard. Also, we could hear mice sliding down the walls of the tent, cars going up and down the nearby road, people talking, and dogs barking.

Later, as we grew older, we got lucky and were able to sleep in the Svobodas' cabin in the back of their yard. One day, the older kids would sleep in the cabin, and then the next day, the younger kids got their turn at a sleepover. One morning, the younger kids got up and decided they should go home and get some eggs and bacon to make breakfast. So, we lit the barrel stove that was in the cabin and everyone went home to get their food. Lo and behold, when we came back, the roof of the cabin was on fire. By the time we put the fire out nobody was hungry anymore. We didn't call the fire department; we just used a garden hose to put the fire out.

We used to build wooden carts to push around for the fun of it. We'd get a board of lumber about five feet long that was ten inches wide and two inches thick and attach two axles and four wheels to it. For steering, we had two sticks on either side of the wheeled buggy. You had a rope hooked up from the sticks to the front end of the buggy to steer it. If you wanted to turn to the right, you'd pull the right stick; to turn left, you'd pull the left stick. We had another stick set up for a brake. You'd pull the stick that was connected to another stick on the back wheels to work as a brake, sort of, if you pulled it hard enough. The bigger and stronger kids pushed the buggies, and the smaller kids got to drive. What a deal!

There was a rusted forty-five-gallon barrel in an old barn near our house that we hung from the rafters and tied four ropes onto its side so we could use it for "bucking" contests. Kids would hold onto the side ropes while one of us mounted the barrel, like bull riding. Thinking back, it was very dangerous if you got hit by the barrel swinging widely because the other kids were always trying to make you fall off the barrel with wild swings. I still don't know what the barn was used for, but it might have had some cows in it at one time.

Each winter, we always made an ice rink where we had a garden in our front yard. We didn't have the valves on taps like we have today, so before we could flood the ice, we had to unthaw the tap by rolling up newspaper and lighting it on fire to thaw it and get water flowing. I don't know how we didn't burn our house down!

Christmas was always a good time when I was a kid, even though we didn't have much money. We always ate well, got some good presents, and had a great Christmas dinner. I always knew what I was going to get for Christmas because I had a brother who went looking in all the usual hiding places. I remember one Christmas when Johnny Ellison, Duane Radford, and I went for a walk down by the old mine and somebody had a pack of Black Cat cigarettes, probably Johnny. Man, we thought we were something, dragging and coughing as we smoked the cigarettes. None of us smoke today!

I used to deliver the *Lethbridge Herald* newspaper in the evenings. Summer was a good time for delivering the paper, but in the winter, if you didn't know when the delivery truck was going to come from Lethbridge in stormy weather, you'd have to wait for him to show up before you could drop off the paper that same night because everyone wanted their paper the day it was published. This was in the 1950s, and I remember a lady by the name of Mrs. Turner giving me a $10 tip for Christmas. Can you imagine how a young kid felt to get that big of a tip? As for collecting money at the end of the month for the papers, I think that my mom and dad paid half of everybody's bill.

Once a month, the old-age pension cheque would come in and we knew that one of our neighbours up the street would be out at the bar. Then one day, while he was coming home from the bar, he somehow got stuck in the picket fence above my house. I was only seven or eight at the time, but with difficulty my friend, Johnny Ellison and I got him off the fence and sent him on his way. When he got to the hill leading up to his house, he'd take one step forward and two steps back. So, Johnny and I got on each side of him and helped guide him to his house. We knocked on the door and, when his wife came, said, "Here's your husband." Before we could turn around, he started to walk out of his house. She yelled at him to get his pants off. Just like that she got out the garden hose and started spraying him off right in front of us. I would have liked to see the looks on our faces as we watched that! That same woman lived to the age of 100 years, and because she was a Montreal Canadiens fan, she got a signed sweater from Guy Lafleur.

When I was a kid, my friends and I used to ride our bikes to the ghost town of Lille for something to do. We'd pick saskatoon berries and raspberries beside the trail, all the way there and back home to Bellevue. We used to drink out of all the little creeks and springs; some places even had rusty old pipes coming out of the ground. We never seemed to get sick from beaver fever, ever. We were also told to get home by five p.m., which we did 100 percent of the time; supper would be ready by then.

We were the first kids to go to Isabelle Sellon School in Blairmore, which was pretty nice, as it was a brand new, modern building that even had a gym with shiny hardwood floors. We'd never had such facilities in our other schools.

Believe it or not, when we were kids, we had four local arenas (one in Bellevue, Blairmore, Coleman, and Hillcrest) and three curling rinks (one in Bellevue, Blairmore, and Coleman). WOW! There were three league hockey teams in my younger years in Bellevue, Blairmore, and Coleman. Each town had its own team, and the players all hated each other.

One time, Duane (author) and I had a moose licence, so we went up the Kananaskis Road on a hunting trip. On the way home, we ran across some fool hens on the side of the road, so we got out of the truck and killed a few birds by throwing rocks and sticks at them. Just as we were getting back into the truck, we heard a shot nearby, and when we came around the corner, we saw two hunters there with what should have been our moose. Oh well, at least we didn't have to do all the work that comes with shooting a moose. As I'm writing this story, I can see three mule deer does eating my lawn—I love that.

Another time, Johnny Ellison, Blythe Mattson, and I went on a drive to Rock Creek, on the east slopes of the Livingstone Range, and spotted a golden eagle that looked like it couldn't take flight. We grabbed a blanket out of the car and threw it over the eagle to bag it. After looking at the talons, we ripped the seat cover off and put that over him too, just in case he got out of the blanket. This was probably all illegal, but we wanted to try to help the bird get better. After driving around for a while, we finally decided what we were going to do with the bird: we very carefully let him out in a field to see if he could fly. All he needed was a place where he could run so he could take off. He wasn't hurt at all, just needed a runway!

I remember one trip where we were in a van going hunting for sharp-tailed grouse when we came across a farm cat chasing a big mallard duck down the road. We stopped and chased the cat away, then picked up the duck and drove around with it all day until we came back to the Passburg (East Hillcrest) Bridge, where we let him out in the Crowsnest River. He swam away happily ever after.

I quit school after Grade 11, while most of the class continued and went on to university to eventually do really well in their lives.

Think of it—we lived during the best time there will ever be in this world!

GROWING UP IN BELLEVUE BY MARILYN COSTIGAN (NEE SVOBODA)

Growing up in our little village of Bellevue offered the best childhood. I lived in a self-contained oasis for the first twelve years of my life before changes came to our town.

Bellevue had everything that we needed. We had our own grocery store, drugstore, Jim's Café, Johnson and Cousens General Store, a post office, Green's Garage, Sickoff's Hardware, Harvey's Hardware store, and the Bellevue Hotel. Bellevue also had its own schools.

We were poor to some people's eyes but very rich compared with other families. We were raised by a wonderful extended family, including our grandparents, Ed and Eva Ledieu, our uncles, aunts, cousins, and, of course, Mom and Dad—Jim and Zena Svoboda. With the involvement of neighbours, each child had at least five or six adults watching over them most of the time.

Some of my best memories are of Christmas concerts at the United Church, family picnics, fishing trips, camping trips, and being able to walk everywhere. There was never any fear of strangers. We played kick-the-can or hide-and-seek on our front street with all the neighbourhood kids. When we were called to supper, we all scattered to our respective homes.

Sometimes, tramps or hobos would come up from the railroad tracks, offering to chop wood or perform some other chore to earn a hot meal. Our parents always treated them generously.

In those days, some services were provided directly to our home. The Rawleigh man would come to our door, selling his wares. Doctor Milton would come to our house when one of us was ill. Everyone looked after each other.

In the winter, Mom would always call to us as we came home from school for lunch to take some of the frozen clothes off the clothesline and stand them up in the house. Before she did the laundry, she would send one of us to check the wind direction, because if the coal mine was working and the wind was blowing from the direction of the mine, she didn't want to hang the clothes on the line until the wind shifted—otherwise, the clothes would turn grey.

COAL TOWN BOYS BY JIM JEPSON

I was born in cosmopolitan London, England, exactly one year after D-Day; my mom was an English war bride and dad a Canadian army volunteer (Clemence de Gude and Harry Jepson). My mother and I arrived by ship in Halifax in April, 1946, and rode the train to Calgary. My dad, who had earlier left England on a troop ship, met us and we proceeded to the bustling hamlet metropolis of Bellevue.

The early years were difficult, to say the least, as the coal mines were not always open, and after he finished high school, my dad's main employment, like so many young men in the Crowsnest Pass, had been mining coal. I have vague memories of our living just a few homes down on the east side of Highway 3, towards Maple Leaf, after turning the corner from Bellevue Motors.

Because of the bleak work prospects and a certain prejudice that came to light later, we left to go back to London where my dad worked on the underground trains for a while. However, the lure of the Pass (my father was born in Frank in 1916) was strong and called him and us back in 1949, so by four years old, I had gone back and forth across "the pond" (the Atlantic) three times.

The annual May Day parade lineup in front of the Bellevue Motors Garage on Main Street. Jim Jepson is in the foreground of the picture with his bike, getting ready for the parade (Photo Credit Jim Jepson).

Upon returning, we stayed for a while in the home that my grandfather had built in the early 1900s, and which we would some years later buy from him for the princely sum of $600, due to my mother's very careful financial money management. That home was on Gertrude Street (now called 215th Street), two blocks south of Main Street, and had a spectacular view of the Frank Slide.

The Bellevue Mine was working again (sort of) and my sister Helene was born in the fall of 1949. Shortly thereafter I met a young lad who would become my oldest and one of my dearest friends, Dennis Amos. As he tells it, I asked him, "Would you like a sweetie?" (English jargon for "candy.") I'm not sure if he knew what I was saying, but when the candy came out, the communication was complete! I was on the way to becoming a Coal Town Kid. Okay for me, not so much for my mum.

As she told me in later life, she found it very difficult during those first years in Bellevue, mostly because of her accent. You see, she had a British accent (I had lost mine on the ship when we first disembarked in Halifax), and as many of the families had a dislike for the British because the "mine bosses" were British, they assumed she was connected to them. This, of course, was wrong. However, she told me that if it hadn't been for the kindness and sincere friendship of a few ladies, she may have packed us up and gone home to England. Those ladies included Sally Amos, Grace Avoledo, Olga Olitch, and Marion Gianino.

The other problem that began to take root was the lure of the local legion and some of the things it represented for my dad. As history has reported, there were many war brides who didn't stick it out, eventually leaving for home in Europe. But my mum was tough when she needed to be and, with help from others, began to make life here better for us. It wasn't long before I was off to Grade 1 at the Bellevue Elementary School on the west end of Main Street. It was a whole new world!

There were lots of kids! Big kids, little kids, all the way up to Grade 12, and a bunch in Grade 1 that I didn't know, but my friend Dennis was there. I soon discovered that the teacher wasn't very kind or nice. I also learned that as we progressed through school, there would be some kids who fit that mould as well. Just as there are bullies now in schools, there were then, particularly as we got into the junior and senior grades and schools merged with other villages and towns. Part of life, I suppose, but being one overshadowed by the opportunity to make more new friends and realizing that there were kind and nice teachers along the way.

Without a doubt, one was Mrs. Isabel Dambois, my Grade 5 and 6 teacher. She was encouraging, challenging, kind, and fair. At the end of Grade 5, she suggested to my parents that I could skip Grade 6 and go on to Grade 7. After discussing this, we decided against it.

Other nice teachers that come to mind were the Isabelle Sellon High School teachers Dave Halton, who taught mathematics, and Reno Bosetti, who taught English and, in later life, became Alberta's Deputy Minister of Education. In addition, I enjoyed Frank Sickoff's classes, as we could get him talking about fishing on occasion and that would be the end of the lesson for that day.

In reflecting back, it struck me that sadly some teachers were "feared" or seemed "unhappy" (based on their countenance) in their roles in the classroom. Perhaps it was because the strap or the ruler over some students' hands, a thrown chalk brush, or other physical punishment was prevalent for, in many situations, the most innocuous offences. These included misspelling a word, talking in class, or in my case, not doing a project exactly the way the Grade 8 shop teacher wanted it. He threw it at me, so I went home in fear of what might be thrown next, but the next day, I was called into the high school principal's office to explain what I thought I was doing leaving class without permission! (No reprimand for the teacher!) However, I recognize, there were times that my behaviour was not proper while growing up, and it has made me ashamed of it. I am truly sorry for that, and pray I might be forgiven by those whom I treated in a less than worthy manner.

We moved a few times after those early years and rented two other homes. One was next to the old hospital, one block north of Gertrude Street, and overlooked the road down to the mine. I remember my older cousin, who had emigrated from England and was interested in television, setting up a tall antenna and hooking up a TV to get reception from CJLH TV in Lethbridge. We got a snowy-filled screen with some figures on it, but it wasn't quite what he had hoped for. A good first try for TV in the Pass, however! The other home was next to the United Church on Main Street. My parents had taken on the jobs of cleaning the church and ensuring that it was heated in the winter (coal and wood were the fuels of the day!). I fixed up the shed in the back of the property to use as a place to "hang out." It was my first foray into carpentry.

Eventually, though, we got back to the home on Gertrude Street on the hill above the Radfords' and Amoses'. This brought some responsibilities for me as I grew older. We had a cellar (no, it wasn't a basement as we think of them today) with a chute from which coal, delivered by truck, came down from outside into the cellar, which we used to keep us warm in winter. The coal had to be piled up and then shovelled into the coal furnace (no gas furnace, thermostat, or central heating in those days) throughout each day and piled in the evening to last all night. Any ashes had to be removed on a regular basis. My job was to ensure that the furnace had enough coal for overnight on many occasions. Also, because the cellar was quite small and needed enlarging, I used five-gallon pails to remove rocks and gravel from around the area, as no formal walls or proper flooring existed. This transpired over many months.

The bonus of Gertrude Street was that it was going to be easier to play street hockey than on the highway in front of our other home! Many of the neighbourhood kids played street hockey before or after supper during the winter. Occasionally on a Saturday, we'd walk all the way down to the old Frank Slide road to a snow-covered slough, clear it off, and put on our skates and play hockey there—where there's a will, there's a way! We weren't allowed to use the Bellevue Arena for pickup games, and hockey wasn't all that well organized in those days. Oh, we did play against the other towns, but the games were generally ad hoc, until one year a coach organized our midget team into a playoff format—and we somehow won. He felt we should purchase jackets as recognition, so the team decided to buy green-and-white jackets with crests and our numbers on them (mine was number eight). We were quite proud of ourselves!

Summer holidays meant camping and fishing trips, and picnics. As we had no other really close relatives nearby, those trips were with friends, like the Amos family, who became like family to us. There's nothing like fresh rainbow or cutthroat trout cooked over an open fire on a cast iron pan, followed by hotdogs roasted on sticks cut from the underbrush!

Ted Amos, Sally Amos, Clem Jepson (back row); Dennis Amos, Jim Jepson, Allan Amos, and Helene Jepson (front row) (Photo Credit: Harry Jepson).

With the mines opening and closing on a fairly regular basis, our vacations, as well as weekends, were enjoying the outdoors of the Kananaskis and Waldron areas or the Castle or Crowsnest rivers, where we could camp, fish, swim, or look for fossils or artifacts. If we were at home, we could hitchhike to Burmis Lake (yes, it was safe to do so in those days) and swim, or we could hike all over the place, or go fishing the Crowsnest River, just down the hill from home, which I was privileged to do on a regular basis, bringing home three or four trout for supper on occasion.

We hiked to Lille once in a while, and in August of 1961, climbed Razorblade Mountain.

Jim Svoboda (L), Allan Amos, Bob Rose, and Tony Stoklosa (R) on top of Razorblade Mountain (Photo Credit: Jim Jepson).

Jim Jepson beside cairn on top of Razorblade Mountain (Photo Credit: Jim Jepson).

There were a host of other kids in our neighbourhood area and in our village (which had grown from a hamlet) whom I got to know as time went by. These included Jim and Larry Svoboda, Don Pagnucco, Duane Radford, Dennis and Larry Quintilio, Johnny Ellison, Tony Stoklosa, and, of course, some of the young ladies: Sylvia Lucchini, Judy Storey, Cathy Beck, Lynn Avoledo, and Marlene Nastasi (among others). It's refreshing to be able to talk with some of these folks and take up right where we left off, even if our paths haven't crossed for a long time. The hospitality that has been shown over the years, particularly by my friend Dennis Amos and until her passing, his dear wife, Patti, is second to none, but others also extend the hand of welcome from time to time. A strong long-standing bond occurred in "the hood" back in those days, I believe.

We did some crazy stuff as kids, like climbing on top of boxcars and running and jumping from one to the next on the siding down by the mine. I tried that and nearly fell between two of them. That ended that caper!

There were no Play Station games or cell phones and so on to keep our thumbs occupied. Instead, we were out and about, using our imaginations and exercising our muscles to keep us "entertained," having harmless fun—for the most part.

In one episode, we were hiking up behind Bellevue to the east, and one of the guys had a hatchet. He had just cut down a diseased small tree; I saw something in the stump and reached in to point it out just as he came down again with the axe. Bad timing on my part! Blood was gushing from my ring finger on my right hand! Everyone's eyes grew as big as saucers as we headed back to town and the doctor's office. All I could think of in my state of shock was whether I would be able to go to the matinee that afternoon, as there was the next installment of a serial before the main movie that I didn't want to miss. The doctor said he could save the tip of my finger without stitches, using bandages and a metal splint, but I had to be very careful for a few weeks. Well, about a week later, I was back in his office, getting told off, and having the splint replaced with a cast. Try and do your school work with a cast on your writing hand! I still bear the scar to this day but have a complete finger thanks to a good doctor's treatment.

Life in Bellevue and the Pass was tough for many, including those who worked the mines of West Canadian Collieries, or later in Vicary Creek in the Kananaskis and other mines, not only because of work stoppages from time to time, but because of the many dangers of mining coal underground. My dad's mine partner died from pneumoconiosis (black lung disease) or silicosis, and others were killed by falling timbers or coal. Safety wasn't always at the top of the list for mine owners, who eyed profits over prevention. These events had a ripple effect on many families over the years. My mum told me years later that in some of the unemployment times, our family lived on $30 per month. I'm not sure how we survived, but I believe it was in part because of the generosity of friends with large gardens, the willingness of local merchants to allow many folks to "put it on the bill" and then pay when they could, and her remarkable money management skills. Prices were not as ridiculously high as they are now, though. A bottle of Pepsi at Jim's Café was $0.10 and you could hang out, play the juke box, and listen to your favourite tunes. Jim Mah, the owner of the café, was very nice.

Without a car for the longest time, my dad finally purchased a 1943 Fargo panel truck. It had front, driver, passenger, and back windows, and "stow and go" seats—a forerunner of the Dodge Caravan, with a slight twist! Sitting behind the driver required lawn chairs; no seat belts back then! Earlier, we relied on the grace of friends when we went on picnics or camping—everyone just piled in.

In 1961, I bought a 1940 Dodge for $33 from Bellevue Motors. The motor didn't work, but the Fargo's motor did and fit. My parents had purchased a slightly newer vehicle by then, so with little mechanical experience, some borrowed how-to books, and Norman Beck's tripod block and tackle, I did a motor exchange. After a bit of tinkering, we got it going! I kept that car until 1999 (I used it for our wedding car in 1967, but did not drive it for all those years).

Bellevue mine car with Turtle Mountain in background (supplied).

Jim's 1940 Dodge with the 1943 Fargo in the background (Photo Credit: Jim Jepson).

In the summer of 1962, I applied for a job with Burmis Lumber Company at their sawmill operation over in the Castle River area. They paid a whopping $1.05/hour! Well, I was hired—on the green chain. For the uninitiated, that's pulling the green cut lumber from the logs (in various sizes from one by four inch to four by six inch) that are travelling along two supported chains, virtually non-stop, and placing them neatly in piles on supports according to their sizes. Once they reach a certain height, a new pile is started for that size. The one by four inch are not heavy, but the four by six inch are! It's back-breaking work. If you get through the first day, you're hired. I did (with a lot of help from Danny Rossi) and was hired. My muscles soon grew on my 140-pound frame.

How did I get to work, you might ask? Out of the kindness of Loretta Hill's dad. He worked there and had a half-ton truck with room in the back for a bunch of us. At around six a.m. every morning, Monday to Friday, we met for our ride, then off through Hillcrest, up the Adanac Road, and over to the mill—rain or shine, freezing or roasting—and home again by six p.m. For the first two weeks, I got home, had supper, and went to bed exhausted. The summer of 1963 was spent at the planing mill down at Burmis on Highway 3, piling dried lumber into dusty boxcars where the temperature was anywhere from 80 to 110°F (27 to 43°C).

Late that summer, I said goodbye to my parents and, other than for visits, left for good for Edmonton and an "inside job" with the Provincial auditor, studying to be a chartered accountant (which didn't pan out, but eventually led to teaching and pension plan administration). Others were leaving for trade schools, colleges, or universities, while some were seeking employment wherever it took them. Our fleeting youth was behind us; we were moving on. Around the corner would hopefully be full-time jobs, perhaps marriage, and maybe even children.

It seems that all of us grew up to be good citizens, with strong character and work ethic—those qualities don't grow on trees.

They're the result of a good, firm upbringing by parents who weathered the storms of two world wars and the Great Depression, the ups and downs and disasters of coal mining, and a fairly tight-knit community, where many looked out for each other's kids, praising them when they were good and letting them and their parents know when they weren't. Three quarters of a century have borne out that things were done right—not perfect, but right.

During the tough times, I occasionally wondered what it would be like to live with Ozzie and Harriet Nelson and their sons, David and Ricky, as portrayed on their radio show. But I know it was too good to be true and make-believe—just a nice escape from time to time. In spite of problems here and there in those days, I'm at peace knowing that I was brought up okay as one of the "Coal Town Kids."

MY CHILDHOOD IN "THE DAIRY" BY TONY STOKLOSA

As we grow old our short-term memory fades or faulters. I have often wondered why my long-term memories are always accessible with total recall. Such would be the case of remembering growing up as a youngster, then a teenager in a coal town called Bellevue in the Crowsnest Pass. We resided on half acre of land in the northwest corner of town in an area locally known as "the Dairy," north of the main street in Bellevue.

My father, whom many called "Hollywood Joe," was an underground coal miner and worked many years at the Briquette Plant at West Canadian Collieries in Bellevue. Our household had no television nor telephone in the 1950s and early 1960s. We were content with CBC Radio and with storytelling around the supper table, as Father would discuss the events of his shift and how he avoided injury time and time again at his hazardous job—all for a salary of $4 a day. You heard right! We also listened to the events of losing this partner or that partner in underground mining accidents.

Sometimes, at exactly six p.m., during supper time, we would hear a siren, loud and clear. This siren resided at the Mine Power House and Fan Station just over the ridge from the Dairy Road ball diamond. This siren sounded like those used in London, England, during World War II to warn citizens of incoming bomb raids. Heard throughout the community, its purpose was to alert the mine employees that there would be no shift to work the following day. All seven of us siblings seated at the table would notice the dismayed look on Mother's face when there would be no $4 earned the next day, as father was the sole bread winner in our family.

Regardless of any hardships, we ate well, as mother was an exceptional cook. All accomplished on a McClary coal and wood stove. Because my folks emigrated from Poland, where many were farmers, we had plenty to eat, as their experience in animal husbandry came with their immigration. We had chickens, rabbits, a hog, a cow (sometimes with calf), and a huge garden that supplied cabbages, potatoes, carrots, beets, turnips, lettuce, and other great produce to eat. Many other Bellevue residents also had barns with cows, chickens, or turkeys, plus gardens—all necessities, as work in the mine was sporadic and not well paying.

As youngsters, much of our entertainment was off in the hills or bush. We built forts, tree houses, and dug pits in the ground to hide and ambush any who might intrude into our domain. Homemade slingshots were the mainstay of our weaponry. The local landfill (dump) was visited often to be scoured for discarded bicycle parts, as most kids had bikes built from scratch. I had built one of these but with some limitations, such as no brakes. One had to ride slowly especially downhill. If anyone had a helmet, it was a found discarded miner's hard hat. Sister Sophie crashed while testing out my creation and broke a leg; I forgot to tell her about the lack of brakes. My lovely Polish-engineered creation met its fate when my enraged father came to the rescue and trashed the thing against the rock pile.

As a youngster, I found a fishing mentor in one of my father's friends, also a coal miner. Lindo Brazzoni was the father of my schoolmate Ernie and his brother, Marcel. Lindo's expertise at catching fish was absolute. When I was able to purchase a fishing pole from Jerry's Sport Shop in Maple Leaf, paid for by monies earned from delivery of newspapers, I was invited to accompany Lindo on a fishing trip to Gold Creek, which flowed through the old townsite of Lille and transited under Highway 3 at Frank to flow into the Crowsnest River. This stream was a fisherman's paradise for rainbow trout and cutthroat trout. The only problem was it was about five miles from home, and we would hike it. Lindo had a two-piece Stout Fly Rod with reel and I a one-piece twelve-foot bamboo rod with no reel; I could not afford one! No matter, a line from the end of the rod to the handle gave me twenty-four feet of reach, almost to the opposite side of any waters of Gold Creek.

I recall one occasion, on a lovely day in June, when I was fourteen years old. My mother had prepared me a lunch in a paper bag, which consisted of a chunk of garlic sausage, a hunk of rye bread, and an apple. The bag with its contents were carried in a white pillowcase. (From lack of a creel, another unaffordable item.) The pillowcase was attached to a pole carried over my shoulder. Lindo packed something similar but in a white flour sack, which, judging from its bulk, may have contained a bottle of dandelion wine. I had a three-foot monofilament leader attached to my line, with a used thermos cork for a strike indicator and three lead sinkers six inch above a #8 bait hook. My bait selections were angle worms (earth worms) and grasshoppers. Lindo used maggots skewered on a #8 brown hackle fly hook.

We set out on foot at six a.m. and arrived two hours later at the confluence of Green Creek and Gold Creek, whence we proceeded to fish downstream. I noticed Lindo pull out a can of snuff and place a pinch under his lower lip. I discovered some time later, that it was maggots that resided under his lower lip. Most of the old-timer fishers did same, the likes of little Mike Sterba, Wingy the Shoemaker, and others. They did not have to mess with a container, which, at times, dropped into the stream. Under the lip was great for quick access when the fish were hot.

As the day wore on, we caught and released many fish. That is to say, we released all that were shorter than fifteen inches. By days end, as we approached Frank, I was having difficulty packing my catch. They were all around two to four pounds and sixteen to twenty-two inches in length. As it was approaching dusk, we decided to head home. Just one mile short of Bellevue, we heard the yapping and yelping of a pack of coyotes, which seemed to be following us. I became uneasy and asked Lindo if we should run for it. He whispered back, "No," as they may attack if they sense fear. He suggested I drop a fish and we would continue.

I reached into my creel (pillowcase) and felt around for a smaller fish, which was about sixteen inches long. I dropped the fish on the ground, and we continued our journey. Shortly after, I asked Lindo why the coyotes were not growling and fighting over the fish. He said to wait a couple of minutes and he would backtrack to see what they were up to. A few minutes had past when Lindo came down the trail with a lit cigarette in his mouth. He said he had not seen nor heard any coyotes. Ten more minutes of walking, and the coyotes started yapping and yelping again.

Lindo instructed me to drop another fish, which I did, and we skedaddled. Two minutes later, Lindo says "You carry on slowly. I have to pee in the bush." After he remerged, we could see the lights of town and were home free. As I bid Lindo good night and thanked him for an awesome day of fishing, I could not help but notice that his flour sack seemed a bit bulkier than when we departed the stream—I was afraid to ask.

It was now dark as I entered the house and found mother pacing the floor with worry. Her countenance brightened as I dumped five large rainbows into the kitchen sink. From that day forward my passion for fishing did not wane to the present.

As I had mentioned earlier, many townsfolk harboured cows, which were released into the wilds after the milking in the morning. Us kids were tasked with locating and herding the cows back home after school was out and before supper time so they could be milked by seven p.m. and stalled. Brother Stan and I, along with Blythe Mattson and Garry Grisak, would head out past the Dairy Road ballpark to the exit tunnel of the Bellevue Mine, which was a place called #2. Here is where we usually found our cow and calf, along with Mike Favaro's cow and Joe Cauville's cows. We had great fun herding the cattle back home. Slingshots were used extensively to keep the herd intact; the mongrel dogs that accompanied us were no border collies. We brought the dogs to fend off the other mongrels, not to mention bears and cougars.

On our way back from one such trip, we spotted a shed in the bush about eighty metres from the mine entrance. As dusk was approaching our curiosity got the better of us. We just had to find out what this shed held. Garry thought it was an outhouse, but it didn't smell like an outhouse; it smelled more of sulphur. We finally got the sheet iron door opened after jimmying two locks. We looked inside but could not see well in the darkened interior. There were several wooden boxes stacked near the back. I asked if anyone had a match. Blythe had a pocket full of Eddy matches that he pilfered from his dad, as he was a prolific smoker. I got a match handed to me, which I struck on the metal wall. We still could not make out what sort of boxes these were. The match soon burned out, so we struck another and looked closer. I dropped the match, then picked it up, as it was still burning. I brought it closer to the top box when we spotted two-inch-tall lettering in black on a pale wooden box. It spelled "Dynamite." Realizing what we had encountered some yelled, "Oh shit, bail out, bail out!"

We ran across the road, and Grisak yelled, "Dive, dive." We all dived into the ditch opposite the road, the same ditch the cows passed through. To our chagrin, these cows were continuously depositing liquid manure as if they were trained to defecate in the ditch and not on the road. After much cursing and shoving each other as to whose bright idea it was to dive into the ditch, and not at all concerned why the dynamite magazine did not explode, we arrived near the bottom of a waterfall that originated from the overflow of the Bellevue water supply reservoir. Under this water fall, we cleaned off as best we could, knowing there would be hell to pay coming home covered in cow shit.

Our town had a pool hall or billiards hall owned and operated by Johnny Quintilio. One had to be sixteen years of age to gain entry to play a game of pool for $0.25. Oftentimes on cold winter nights, some of us under sixteen years would hang out behind the large windows and watch the games inside. At times, John Q., as he was called, invited us in out of the wind and -30°F degree nights to sit by the huge potbelly coal stove, which glowed red hot. Here, we would listen with fascination to stories of hunting wildlife from the likes of Vince Bosetti, Frank Houda, Pete Gianino (Marion's husband) and Roy Derome. It was from this fascination of related hunting experience that I discovered my second mentors. What I learned and remembered from these stories launched my hunting career.

At the age of sixteen, I purchased for $16 a .303 British Lee-Enfield rifle, paid for with earnings from employ as a milkman's helper. The rifle was purchased through the Army & Navy catalogue out of Winnipeg, Manitoba. A box of cartridges was purchased for $5 from Bill Sickoff's hardware store.

My first hunting excursion started in early September. I set off on foot from home to the South Livingstone Range to a place called Lester's Valley. I had a hunting licence for two antlered mule deer (bucks). As I trekked up Lester's Valley, I encountered mule deer tracks in two inches of snow and figured there were at least seven bucks in this herd. I pursued this herd up and over the mountain to the side of Gold Creek Valley. About 100 metres ahead, I spotted my quarry in the fog. It was hard to get a good bead through peep sites, so I opened fire. Deer were running every which way. After emptying my ten-round magazine, I crossed over and found two great mule bucks expired. I quickly gutted them as instructed months earlier by my mentors, then headed back to town to get help in recovery. I contacted Albert Truant and his brother Johnny for assistance. They agreed, and I was picked up at four p.m. by Johnny in his Willys Jeep. I chose these lads, as they were renowned as great hunters and outdoorsmen.

By the time we climbed almost to the top of the mountain, it was getting late, but we located the mule deer and proceeded to drag them down the mountain. Johnny stopped partway down and exclaimed there was another dead buck, a third, in the gulley. Albert was furious and exclaimed I was only allowed a limit of two. I sheepishly explained it was foggy and spotting through peep sites must have made me lose track. The Truant boys dragged all three deer to the jeep, we loaded them up, and set off for home to drop off two deer for me. Johnny said they would contact the game warden and deliver a found dead wildlife.

BELLEVUE "GANGS" BY GEORGE DOWSON

Most everyone has heard of a gang—the Jessie James gang, the Dalton gang—but until now, most have never heard of the gangs from Bellevue. There were Roy's gang, Bob's gang, Doug's gang—hell, there was even a couple of girl's gangs.

In 1952, I was twelve and a member of Doug's gang. In order to be in Doug's gang, you either could do one of two things: pay $0.05 and be in, or go through an initiation. There were six of us, including Doug, and only one, Bill, was not willing to part with $0.05—he opted to be initiated. Bill had a paper route; I believe he delivered the *Toronto Star Weekly*, if memory serves, so it wasn't that moneybags couldn't afford it. Bill figured if he had to spend $0.05, he would buy something he loved—something like fifteen jaw breakers.

So, the initiation was set for Saturday morning at ten thirty a.m., at the Bellevue Dairy Road ballfield. When Saturday morning finally arrived, everyone was a bit early, except for Doug. When he finally arrived, he took two things from his basket on his bike—a slingshot and an apple—which meant medieval times were about to begin. All the action took place at home plate: Bill was to stand very, very still with the apple on his head, while Doug did his ritual of checking the slingshot, checking the wind direction, and taking steps sideways, then forward. This went on for a few minutes till finally Doug brought the slingshot to eye level, pulled back, and let go.

All I heard was a dull thud—the apple had fallen to the ground and so did Bill. I immediately ran to Bill, and when I looked around, Sir Doug and his merry men had vanished. I stayed because Bill and I had grown up together; we lived a few houses apart and we were good friends. I honestly thought he was dead, and all I could do was scream at him for not paying the $0.05. I was really in panic mode when finally, his moans and groans brought me back down to earth. Bill was trying to get up, and I helped him get to a bench to sit down.

The rock had nailed him right between the peepers, and he was sporting an impressive goose egg. He would no doubt be the talk of the school on Monday morning. After a few minutes, Bill got up, picked up the apple that had fallen by home plate and headed home. He told me later that he was proud that he didn't have to pay the $0.05 and he also got a free apple out of the deal.

PARADISE IN THE ROCKY MOUNTAINS OF ALBERTA BY JIM SVOBODA

I was born in Frank, Alberta, March 16, 1944. My family moved to Bellevue in 1950. My early memories are of me at four or five years old trying to keep up with my father while he checked his trapline along the Crowsnest River in Frank—almost always in the snow, but I loved it!

Bellevue was a great place to be a kid. From my home, within just a two- or three-minutes' walk in any direction, I could find one of my good close friends. There were perhaps ten or twelve, maybe more, boys my age. Girls too! After school (I didn't mind school and actually kind of liked it), I hung out with a few and sometimes many friends, like Jimmy Radford, Chuck and Dennis, Jimmy Jepson, Bobby Storey, Doug Melson, and Cyril McDonald. We were almost always outside, enjoying time spent hiking, biking, fishing, hunting, and playing all kinds of sports. But we mostly just goofed around, hanging out on Main Street. My nickname was Sibby: "Svo" was hard for my friends to say, so they said, "Siboda," which I guess it became Sibby.

In those days, the main highway (Highway 3) came right through the middle of town, so there were lots of vehicles to see, and I'd dream that someday maybe I would be one of those drivers (LOL). We had such fun on Main Street. We would pour a line of water across the road so it looked like a rope lying there in the early evening shadows. Five or six of us would each stand on either side of the street and wait for a vehicle to come; when the vehicle got close, we would all yell, "Pull," and make a pulling motion. We loved the sound of the tires braking as we all ran like hell.

Another prank I remember (usually led by at Tommy Woodward or Wynn Ellison) is we would get a small box, fill it with horse poop or dog poop, and wrap it in nice Christmas or birthday paper with a ribbon. We would place it full view of the cars coming by. Many drivers would stop, pick it up, and take it home. Others would open it, curse, and kick it into the ditch.

Home life was great. Mom and Dad were always there when we needed them. We were poor but didn't know it then. Living off the land was never truer than it was for my family. Dad fished every day he was able to. We had a big vegetable garden in the backyard. When I turned twelve, my father gave me a Cooey single-shot .22 calibre rifle; I carried it all over town—can you imagine that in today's tight-assed society? I still have it today. Dad would often trade his freshly caught fish to the local Hutterites for their eggs and chickens. We'd eat trout, Rocky Mountain Whitefish, deer, elk, moose, wild mushrooms, blueberries, rabbit stew, grouse, and pheasants—even black bear. I remember Garry Grisak once coming to my home in my teenage years while my dad was frying some meat. Garry tried some and said, "Wow, this is really good. What is it?" My dad said, "Black bear." Garry still does not believe it.

My brother and two sisters now live in the Edmonton area, while I live in Calgary, and my sister Lori in Kamloops, BC. Sister Linda and her husband, Don Harvey, still live in Bellevue—bless them! They have to put up with us at their home whenever we visit. We all still refer to Bellevue as home. Yup, we say, "Goin' down home for the weekend."

A VISIT TO THE LOCAL DENTIST

It's no wonder I would never follow my mother's dream that I'd become a dentist. She'd always tell me what great jobs dentists had and how much money they made. "You could be rich," she used to say, "and work in a nice clean office all day."

I had so many unpleasant experiences with Dr. R. B. (Bob) Burgman, the local dentist, that I dreaded the thought of ever being a dentist myself and inflicting what I considered torture on patients. Not that Dr. Burgman was a poor dentist or a bad person, to the contrary; from all reports, he was a gentleman and a fine person, highly respected in the community. It was just the dental equipment of the day was so primitive that I absolutely dreaded a visit to his office.

My phobias had nothing at all to do with Dr. Burgman, per se. Also, it probably didn't help that my mother needed assistance from one of her sisters to literally drag my brother, Jimmy, up the stairs to his office. Seriously, it was so bad, he had to be literally dragged by his feet to the dentist's office. This didn't make me feel any more at ease and just added to my apprehension. I'm not sure I really set the stage for a good visit to the local dentist either when I used to sing, "Dr. Burgman is a lady; he's wearing white shoes"—repeated a few times for good measure while stringing out the *y* in "lady" to sound like an *e* for as long as possible. As was the custom of the day, dentists dressed in white garb with white shoes.

"There, there, my boy," he used to say as I settled in for my examination. "Let's see what we have here today. Have you been brushing your teeth regularly? You sure seem to have a lot of plaque again." These were the days before dental floss arrived on the scene. I would squirm and shiver as he probed my mouth looking for the dreaded cavities, or a loose tooth, in his antiseptic office. "Keep your mouth wide open, and don't you dare bite me!" he snapped. Sheesh, so much for friendly chatter!

"You have to brush your teeth at least twice a day, Duane, and always after drinking pop and eating candy, or your teeth will rot," he would repeat many times. How many times did he tell me the same thing? I had visions of rotten black teeth and then no teeth at all, like a beggar. *How could people eat with no teeth?* I wondered. The stories I had heard about dentures made me break out in a cold sweat. There was no way I wanted dentures.

Whenever I visited the dentist, I couldn't help but think of a Bellevue resident locally known as "Louis" by townsfolk. Louis was an old bachelor, one of a few taxi drivers in town. He lived like a hermit behind the Canada Post Office on Main Street, in what can only be described as a fire trap and a junk yard. He would fit today's definition of an incurable hoarder. Louis only had one tooth that I could make out anyway: an upper front incisor that made him look like a walrus. I'm sure that Louis never saw a dentist in his whole life. He was widely regarded as a cheapskate and was a regular at the Saturday afternoon matinee with all the kids in town because it was inexpensive. For $0.25 you could get into the show and buy a pop and popcorn. It only cost $0.10 to get into the matinee in Bellevue in the 1950s.

Getting a cavity filled was only slightly better than the thought of going before a firing squad. I was terrified of these visits to Dr. Burgman. He would start by saying, "Now, Duane, I don't think you'll need any freezing today, will you? It will only take more time and you're a big boy now, aren't you? Let's just skip the freezing and give it a try." I'd tell my mom not to leave the waiting room, just in case I needed her. There was no way I wanted freezing unless it was absolutely necessary. Dr. Burgman had a needle the size of a small baseball bat that he used to give shots of freezing. Just the frightening sight of this needle was all it took to say, "No thanks!"

Next, he would start the dentist's drill. There were rather lengthy rubber bands and pulleys with little motors that made the drill go around. It was not what you would call a high-speed drill by any stretch of the imagination. The bright dental lamp shone down hard on my face, more or less blinding me. How could you help but not squint? Shortly, an ominous sound of a drill would reverberate through the clinic, a scary whirring noise. Once in a while Dr. Burgman would stop and ask me to spit out the tooth material. He'd squirt in some water to rinse my mouth. I needed these breaks; they were the only time that I dared to breath. It wasn't unusual to see smoke coming out of your mouth—no, I'm not kidding! Then there would be more white-knuckle waiting as he started the drill again.

Once I winced, only to be given a hard slap in the face. Corporal punishment went beyond the school classroom in those days. "Hold still, Duane! For crying out loud, how do you expect me to fix the cavity with you jumping all over?" he cried out. This kind of rough behaviour would have been good for a major lawsuit today, but at that time, kids did what they were told. The acrid smell of burnt teeth was almost bad enough to make me sick; it was nauseating. Periodically, Dr. Burgman would stop for a while and hose down my mouth. After the slap, I didn't dare move a muscle.

I could see a bottle clearly labelled chloroform on the counter in a dental cabinet and had visions of the dentist putting me out for good if I didn't behave. I had heard lots of rumours about patients who never came to again after getting the chloroform treatment. I think Dr. Burgman only used it in extreme cases, maybe if you had deep roots that just wouldn't let go. When he yanked out a tooth, he would practically stand on the dental chair as he yanked it out. Without exaggerating, there would be blood all over the place—seriously, that's the truth. "There, there, now that wasn't that bad, was it, Duane?" he used to say. Dr. Burgman was also fond of saying, "If you would sit still for a minute, I'll be finished a lot faster." Finally, the job would be done, and I'd get to spit out the lumps of waste filling, blood, and this dreadful buildup of foul-tasting saliva in a dental sink. If I was good, my reward was a toothbrush. If I misbehaved, I'd have to listen to Dr. Burgman wail to my mother about what a cry baby I'd been and how he didn't want to see me again until I grew up, which actually wouldn't have bothered me.

THE TENT BY GEORGE DOWSON

Growing up with an older brother was not the highlight of my younger days, even though some days now, I really miss him. My brother, Tom, was sixteen and I was ten, so if there were places that required an adult present, Tom would be asked, bribed, or paid to take me with him.

Every year, my uncle Matty and his friends would spend a week fishing at a place called the Race Horse (a creek in the Kananaskis Valley). My uncle would bring his tent down to our place and set it up a week before to air the tent out. The tent was huge and slept six people. One night before the weekend, my brother asked if he and two friends could sleep in the tent on Friday and Saturday night. Both my parents agreed to it, but when I asked about joining my brother and his friends in the tent too, I got an emphatic "NO" from my brother. I heard, "You're too young" from my mom and "Listen to your mother" from my dad. I did not take rejection easily, and my mind went into overdrive to get even with the emphatic "NO" I had received.

Now, I had heard somewhere that if you rub the inside of the tent roof with your hand, it would leak, but not knowing if that was fact or fiction, I took one of my mom's sewing needles just for extra insurance. When I was finished, the palms of my hands were sore from rubbing and there were also a couple hundred little pinholes in the tent's roof. If I had known the rain dance moves, I would have done that too.

Friday night came and went without incident. Was my plan and all that hard work for nothing? I also knew if I helped the plan and got caught, my behind would pay for it. Well, I went to bed wondering if my plan would work or if it was doomed. I got my answer about two a.m., when the first clap of thunder shook the house, and a couple of minutes later, rain was pounding on the shingles on the house. I listened intently until I heard the porch door open and three soggy people walked in. God had answered my prayers! Mom got them all dried off and into fresh, dry PJs. One slept in my brother's room, one slept on the couch, and when my brother walked into my room to sleep there, he got the emphatic "NO" and had to sleep on the floor. Revenge is sweet!

GROWING UP IN "MAPLE LEAF" BY LAWRENCE KRYZANOWSKI

Like many interprovincial migrants to Alberta, I was born in Saskatchewan. A few years after my father died when I was a toddler, my mother moved to the Pass with myself and my older brother Julian Roman (Julius). My mother remarried a coal miner, Steve, who was also an interprovincial migrant from Saskatchewan that I became very close to. My brother received the nickname "Julius Caesar" or "Caesar" for short, and for many today, they believe Caesar is his first name. My friends called me by my nickname: Krizan.

I grew up during the 1950s and 1960s in our one-story house that was situated in the community of Maple Leaf, which became part of the village of Bellevue in 1957. The house was located on the north side of what is now the intersection of 223 Street before 30th Avenue. Our community was ethnically diverse (Ukrainians, Poles, Italians, Slovaks, Czechs, English, Scots, and Irish) with most fathers working or having had worked in the coal mines. Thus, we had many close friends and schoolmates that came from different ethnic and linguistic backgrounds.

The same applied to store proprietors. To illustrate, Joe Mah's Bellevue Café was a local hangout reached after a long walk of over a mile across and along the major Highway 3 that meets the Trans-Canada Highway 1 at Hope, BC. The café was also a place where you could buy three single vinyl records for $1 after the records in the jukebox were changed. Ozar's (Mike's) service station at the corner of our block was also a frequent hangout for adults and teenagers, where you could "shoot the breeze" for hours and have a pop, ice cream, or consume what is now considered junk food.

Unemployment was very high at times due to the openings and closings of some mines and reduced workweeks for many of the mines that did not close. There was a persistent absence of any meaningful provincial or federal support for the community. The Pass was then considered the forgotten part of Alberta. The real estate scars of the boom and bust of coal mining were evident in our community. There was a vacant house on the other side of the street in which we played hide-and-seek. Within a short walk, there were many blocks of empty houses and empty lots due to house relocations that followed the up-the-street mine closure during an earlier period.

During the tough times, cabbage soup was a staple. During one long period when my stepfather worked only one or two days a week while many others were unemployed, he worked in the fields for a Mennonite community near Pincher Creek. As a barter transaction, he received some produce from the land as his payment. In one case, the payment included a pig that we butchered, salted, and smoked. This taught me how to carve, which has been useful to this day.

Maple Leaf had no sewage or water utilities, so a good part of my early life involved the use of the outhouse for necessary bodily functions and the outdoor hand pump that sometimes needed to be unfrozen to get water. Newspapers and catalogues from Eaton's and Simpson's played a dual role from a means to purchase items to serving various bodily functions in these outhouses.

Various food items were stored in the well, in lieu of modern refrigeration. The food was put in a bucket and was lowered and raised with a rope into the well. Although such activities were sometimes challenging during Alberta's cold winters, they were an excellent preparatory experience for the future and the need to be positive and self-reliant.

Our four-room house, however, continually improved (slowly) through hard work, without any government support. We first dug the basement, put in cement walls and floor, and inserted a coal/wood burning furnace that augmented the coal/wood burning stove in the kitchen. The stove served the dual purpose of cooking and heating. Digging the basement was tough, as the soil was clay and it needed to be spread on the side and front areas of our house. Much later, we added in-house plumbing and a bathroom that required the installation of an outdoor septic holding tank, which could not be close to our ground water supply. Between those changes, the full-length veranda in the front of the house was sacrificed to extend both the master bedroom and the living/dining room by about six-feet each.

The garage was of a good size. We had a car as long as I could remember. As a teenager, I was able to use the car. My stepfather decided to repaint the Buick pink and black so it was visually easy to identify. The car was popular with my friends because, according to my close friend Ken, it was the only car with a radio that our group had access to.

After working for a mechanic, situated near our house, one summer, we received an old car (four-door Hudson, I think) that had to be pushed to start. There was no trouble getting a gang of kids of various ages to help with the pushing. After the car was started and rolling, the gang jumped in and we went for a ride. One day, we decided to follow the old Lille ghost mountain trail, and the car got stuck in an old creek bed. Our neighbor who had a two- or three-ton truck took hours and much cursing to pull the car out of that creek bed.

Our family had to be self-reliant. There was a barn in our double lot, where chickens and even a pig were raised. Most of the rest of the yard was used to grow vegetables. We also planted potatoes on close proximity lots when such opportunities were available. One of my responsibilities was to look after the gardens.

When TV arrived, we had one channel from Lethbridge, which had poor and intermittent reception. Often, it looked like there was a snow blizzard on the screen. Radio reception was better. Since we were close to the U.S., many rock 'n' roll stations with the latest hits could be listened to. I remember watching with disbelief the blurry images on the TV after arriving from school for a noon break on Friday, November 22, 1963, when John F. Kennedy was assassinated.

I remember many walks in the scenic mountains a few blocks from home and the location of the non-operating mine (Mohawk

Bituminous Mine, I believe). In a short time, you were moving quickly up the mountain from where there was an excellent view of the famous Frank Slide of 1903. It also was a good area for picking red-top mushrooms and harvesting some wild game.

Fishing and outdoor activities during the summer and hockey during the winter when the local arena was open were fantastic. During the summer, Julius and I would catch our daily limit of trout (rainbow, browns) and/or Rocky Mountain whitefish from the Crowsnest River in the valley between Bellevue and Hillcrest. We enjoyed dry fly fishing while walking down the middle of the river or bait fishing using grasshoppers, marshmallows, maggots, earth worms, salmon eggs, and so on. At some point each summer, it became difficult to give the fish away, as possible recipients of the fish, like our family, also had their fill. Looking back, it is not obvious that the fish were totally safe because some coal and sludge from the Bellevue Mine that was piled by the river ended up in the river. I also remember being woken up at about three a.m. often by my brother and his late friend Johnny so that after a two- or so-hour drive northward (North Fork), we could fish at the crack of dawn. Johnny's nickname was "Muscles," even though he was far from being muscular. I remember good experiences from very friendly hockey games against various teams, including ones from Alberta's First Nations (e.g., Blood 148 Reserve near Cardston, Alberta, and the Piikani 147 Reserve near Brocket, Alberta).

Since our barn faced the back alley, it was great for someone who loved hockey. I would spend hours every day in the winter shooting a puck against the wall. During most evenings, we would play street hockey until at least ten p.m. While I played a lot of organized hockey in those years, this was interrupted by periods when the arena in Bellevue was not operational. Generally, I was a first-line centre, and we won a number of championships.

I enjoyed swimming, but with no available community centre, this was done in one of the lakes. It involved either hitching a ride from strangers on Highway 3 or cycling on that highway. The closest and easiest to reach was Burmis Lake, where we could dive off the rocks into the deep end of the lake. Later, when car access became available, I would drive to the larger Lee Lake, where you could swim many miles back and forth across the lake.

My spending money came from delivering newspapers (*Lethbridge Herald* and *Calgary Daily Herald*) and tying fly hooks that my step-father sold for me. Since my paper routes were many miles in length and spread out, my bike was the mode of transportation even in the winter. Lunch bucket chains were put on the wheels of the bike to increase the traction. All bike repairs were done by *moi* in-house, such as putting a hot or cold patch on the inner tire tube or replacing links in a broken bike chain.

Unlike my mother, who had attended high school, my stepfather had almost no formal education. As the need arose, I tried to teach my stepfather how to read and helped him verify his birthdate. After a prolonged exchange of letters with the appropriate government department in Saskatchewan, we were informed by mail that they did not have a definitive birthdate, although he was born in that province. Based on their advice, we made a choice from a few possible dates. This was not a unique experience, since I had a similar experience trying to get information about my late father, who was also born in Saskatchewan.

Our holiday season was always a long one with two Christmases and two New Years. Lots of very late nights, and talk, food, and drink at home and when we made the rounds visiting those we knew. Food included fish, duck, turkey or goose, *kutia* (sweet grain pudding), *borsch* (beetroot soup), *varenyky* (dumplings filled with mashed potatoes or cabbage or cottage cheese or whatever) and *golubtsi* (cabbage or beet leaf rolls stuffed with minced meat and rice) topped with sour cream.

My elementary schooling was a walk to the Maple Leaf School, and then a daily school bus ride to the Hillcrest School for the junior grades and Isabelle Sellon High School in Blairmore thereafter. I especially liked the recess periods, when we could play softball or football where I could quarterback. I was fortunate that I could get top grades without really much effort, which allowed me to have more fun. The one exception was French language, where I worked hard but with very little success. My English teacher in Grade 10 was instrumental in encouraging me to write, which culminated in a second prize in a province-wide essay competition. It was an honour to be the high school president in my Grade 12 academic year before I went to university.

To fund my undergraduate studies, and given very limited employment opportunities, I worked the summers of 1964, 1965, and 1966 far underground at the Vicary Mine for Coleman Collieries Ltd. in bucking coal (pushing coal from the face, down the chutes to the cars below), timber packing (bringing heavy and long green logs up the slope with a partner to the mine face to support the ceiling), and roof bolting (drilling holes into the unsupported roof and then inserting a roof bolt to better secure the roof). The hiring boss did not want to hire someone for the summer, so the first year, he heard me ask repeatedly for a job when he arrived early in the morning and when he finished his shift late in the day. After about one week to ten days, he said that anyone who wants a job that badly can start tomorrow.

I worked all the different types of shifts: day, afternoon, and night. The conditions were such that there was total darkness if the lamp on your hard hat was off. Mid-shift meals were at the worksite and eaten when your face and hands were completely black from the coal dust. It sure felt great to have the hot shower at shift's end before taking the bus back to civilization. The daily pay was $17.35 the first summer, and $17.75 the third summer. Not that far above today's minimum hourly wage of $15 in Alberta and Ontario. I was fortunate that I did not have a broken or damaged body part or a respiratory ailment (e.g., black lung) like every mine worker that

I've met. Many miners also were killed in the mines, including my stepfather, who had many work-related injuries and was killed along with others in a mine flood and cave-in in 1969.

Reflecting, behaviour is determined by genes and environment. Having hardships mixed with pleasurable moments teaches you the importance of a good education and of being self-reliant, independent, forward-looking, focused, and tolerant.

MEMORIES OF CHRISTMAS IN BLAIRMORE BY LOUISE COSTIGAN-KERNS

Christmastime in Blairmore was magical, filled with wonderful food and comradery. We had generous neighbours and friends who were from many different countries. They brought their traditions to our community and enriched all of our lives.

I have vivid memories of my childhood at Christmastime. On Christmas Eve, I remember my mother insisting that I go to bed early, right after dinner, because of Midnight Mass. I would lie in bed too excited to sleep, listening to my dad's Christmas music on CBC radio, before I'd get up around eleven p.m. I only learned when I went to college that the music my dad listened to was Handel's famous *Messiah*; I knew most of it just from listening!

Midnight Mass at the Catholic Church was very special. My mother and the choir members worked hard to make the music memorable every year. She played the organ for the service. There were wonderful singers, like Eric Price, who was a former principal of the Isabelle Sellon School. Eric had a beautiful, natural tenor voice. He would always sing "O Holy Night," and it was inspiring. When I was in junior high and high school, I would often sing a duet ("Do you hear what I hear?") with Bonnie Jean Dobek. Bonnie-Jean also had a beautiful, natural voice.

After mass, we would head over to my grandparent's house, where my grandmother had prepared an Italian antipasto tray, with salami, cheeses, and olives, and always partnered with something good to drink. We would finish around one thirty a.m. I was excited to get home because my parents would let us open the stockings that we had hung on the fireplace in the living room. Santa always managed to come while we were at church.

When I was little, I slept in our den. My parents always set up the Christmas tree there. I loved going to sleep with the lights on and was especially fascinated by the bubbler lights. My dad would often curse the bubblers, as they were very finicky and sometimes would not bubble or light up at all! Magically, on Christmas morning, I would wake up and there would be presents under the tree. My parents must have been very quiet! I must have been a heavy sleeper, as I always missed Santa's arrival.

Wonderful foods were always a part of Christmas. Before Christmas Day, one of my grandparent's friends, Mrs. Drew, would deliver a platter of beautifully handmade Christmas cookies. I can't imagine how she made so many different types without a freezer. Our neighbour, Mrs. Costanzo was a short Italian lady who had a big heart. A conversation with her would be a mix of mostly Italian, with a few English words sprinkled in. I would usually just nod and smile until I studied Italian in college; when I returned, I was able to understand our conversations much better! Mrs. Costanzo was an amazing cook. She would often appear at our door with a plate filled with large, light white crispy buns. At Christmastime, she made a traditional Italian sweet bread called *pita piena* (full bread). It was a sweet bread filled with raisins, currents, and sometimes nuts. We would have it Christmas morning with mandarin oranges, and it was delicious.

My family and Blairmore are always in my heart at Christmas. It was a wonderful place to grow up, and I will never forget it! It also helped me appreciate the special qualities of so many different cultures and people.

CHRISTMAS IN BLAIRMORE BY PETER COSTIGAN

Like all the communities in the Crowsnest Pass, Blairmore was a close-knit community, where everyone knew their neighbours and neighbours looked out for each other. The population of the Crowsnest Pass was multicultural, and all lived in harmony.

The Crowsnest Pass was essentially a mining community. Miners immigrated from all over Europe to work in the coal mines in the Pass. There were miners from Wales, Poland, Italy, Czechoslovakia, and elsewhere. The Welsh and Italian miners were famous for their fine, tenor singing voices.

On Christmas morning, our Italian neighbour, Mrs. Costanzo, would ring our doorbell and present us with fresh Christmas baking. Later in the morning, the miner's male choir would go door to door singing Christmas carols. At each house, they were invited in for a drink. Unfortunately, if your house was one of the ones they reached later in the morning, the choir's voices were slurred.

It was a tradition to visit your friends on Christmas Day; we called it "making the rounds." At each house, we were offered a drink and some special Christmas food. Sometimes, we were slightly inebriated by the time we returned home for dinner. I remember sitting at the dinner table in the living room and looking out the window to see my brother David dancing under a street lamp as he made his way home from making the rounds.

My Italian grandparents, Serafino and Margaret Trono, owned a jewellery store in Blairmore. They would keep the store open late on Christmas Eve to accommodate the schedules of the miners, who might be working night shifts. After they closed the store, they would join us for Christmas Eve dinner, and after dinner, we would all go to Midnight Mass. My mother, Beatrice Costigan, a pianist and music teacher, would play the organ to accompany the church choir in singing Christmas carols. There were many fine voices in the choir. My father, Thomas Costigan QC, sang in the choir.

My brother and I were altar boys, and we would assist the priest during the Mass. After Mass, we would stop at our grandparent's house for more food and another drink.

This Christmas spirit was emblematic of the culture in the Pass. Everyone was friendly and trusting. No one locked their doors.

4

WINTER IN THE PASS

THE MOUSETRAP

Unless you grew up in the country prior to the 1960s, you likely never had to put up with mice in your house. They were a fact of life for country folk when I was a kid. They were a nuisance, leaving their droppings all over a house. Winter was the worst time for mice in our house in Bellevue. However, there was no telling just when you might be invaded by these pesky rodents. There would be the telltale signs, such as little black droppings on the kitchen floor. Mice knew where to find food and would head for cupboards in the kitchen or the panty in the basement. I don't know how many mice I trapped in the basement panty, but it was likely in the hundreds, a never-ending job. There was no keeping them out of the house because they could crawl under the basement garage door. Every autumn, it seemed that we would be overrun with mice and mice trapping season would really begin in earnest. Mind you, a family of mice could take up residence during any time of the year and were masters at evading the occupants paying the rent.

We used a standard wooden mousetrap with a spring wire frame to catch mice. This kind of mousetrap has been around for a long time. You'd bait the trap with a piece of Velveeta cheese and then pull the wire frame back and set it in a small notch in the trap. When a mouse tried to eat the baited cheese, it would set loose the wire frame, which would spring back and crush the mouse's neck.

Sometimes, it crushed their skull. If a mouse was really fast, it might break their back as they tried to get away. Once in a while, you might even catch one by the tail. The traps rarely failed, and sometimes, I'd catch two or three mice in a single night. The dead mice would be cremated in the furnace next to the pantry, because we had this vague feeling, they might be carrying the plaque—germs for sure. In those days, all microbes were categorized as "germs," a catchall for bacteria and viruses.

Mom used to delegate this trapping operation to me whenever she felt that mice were in the house. It seemed that this could go on for months on end, but early winter was always prime trapping time. The war on mice was unrelenting until none could be trapped for several nights in a row. Then, you could be pretty sure that they were all gone. Many families had cats as a second line of defence, and we also had one for a few years too. Our cat's name was Suzy, but she wasn't much of a mouser, and I probably caught as many or more mice as she did.

One winter, the mice were really bad and were in our kitchen just about every night. Shortly after the lights went out, you could hear the pitter patter of their little feet on the kitchen linoleum. Try as we might, they wouldn't go for the cheese in the mousetraps set strategically around the kitchen. This was hard to comprehend because mice are very fond of cheese. No end of trapping produced any results, though, and I was at a loss over what to do. Undaunted, I switched tactics and decided to wait until the mice came into our kitchen at night and try to find out where they were hiding. It didn't take long for the mice to appear after the lights went out. I could hear them running in the kitchen that was beside my bedroom. I carefully left my room and quietly walked over to the light switch. Not a creature was stirring. They must have sensed that I was in the room and froze. When I switched on the light, there was a moment of silence and then all hell broke loose.

Several mice came out of the bottom of the garbage can beside the stove. We had one of those chrome-covered garbage cans with a lid that flipped opened if you put your foot on a hinged floor plate on the bottom of the garbage pail. This foot plate was in a small opening on the front of the garbage pail, and this was their escape hatch and where they got into the garbage pail. No wonder they weren't going for the cheese. They had a buffet every night in the garbage pail. The pail wouldn't be emptied until the morning, so they had their choice of leftovers from the whole day to feast on. After they bolted from the garbage pail, they made a beeline for some holes in the floor behind the pail that had been cut for some plumbing from the basement. It was just like a fire hall! They would slide down the pipes to the basement and safety!

These mice were no dummies and were great at evading me. I'd have to come with another strategy if I was ever going to catch them. Their weakness was their habit of coming up the pipes each night. They must have known that it was safe when the lights went out, and they could tell when to move by watching the holes cut for the pipes in the kitchen. If it was dark, everyone would be in bed—or so they thought. I waited until the next night to spring my trap. Sure enough, a few minutes after the lights in the kitchen were turned off, the mice were back at it on their garbage forays. I could hear them scurrying around the kitchen, making their way towards the garbage pail.

This time, however, I was ready for them. I had an empty plastic bread bag in my hand. I tiptoed to the light switch and flicked the light on. There was dead silence as the mice sensed my presence. Slowly, I crept toward the garbage pail. Next, I put the plastic bag over the opening in the bottom of the pail. Then I rattled the metal garbage pail and waited. It didn't take the mice long to try to make their escape. Out they dashed, right into the plastic bread bag. I had three chubby, fine-looking specimens all trying to figure out what had gone wrong as they tried to find some purchase on the side of bag. This was better than those old-fashioned mousetraps! It took a few days to catch all who had invaded our house, but when it was over, there was no more pitter patter of little feet when the lights went out and we could rest at ease.

WHAT'S THAT SMELL, DUANE?

I was in charge of attending to the coal furnace and keeping the home fires burning during the winter months. This was no small job, because if you weren't careful and it got too cold, the pipes inside the house would freeze and there would be no water. This was in the days before natural gas furnaces and thermostats. A cold house was one thing, but frozen water pipes were really bad news. Unfortunately, being the number one furnace attendant meant I had to be one of the first to rise to make sure that there was heat in the house in the morning.

There is nothing quite like a coal stove or furnace to heat a home. I don't know why, but there is just something different than the heat from natural gas furnaces. Coal fires give off a penetrating, comfortable heat that can only be described as luxurious and comforting.

In addition to keeping the furnace going, I also had to take out the coal ashes, usually daily, or the furnace wouldn't work properly for lack of air circulation. This was always a messy job, as it was impossible to scoop out the ashes without spilling them and creating a lot of fine dust. Once the ashes were in the ash bin, they would be taken outside and piled in a spot set aside just for this purpose, near the garbage barrel. My dad had a contract with the town to pick up local garbage. The contract also required him to pick up coal ashes. I used to help my brother, Jimmy, do this during the summer. We'd pick up the ashes with the aid of a front-end loader and scoop shovel. My job was to shovel the ashes into the bucket of the front-end loader that he couldn't pick up. I always hoped that it would be calm on the days we did this because the ashes would really irritate my eyes on windy days.

Most nights, I would make sure that I banked the furnace before I went to bed because it was a real pain in the neck to start when the fire went out. I would check to make sure that there were enough chunks of coal in the furnace to burn all night long. If you put in too many, you might light the house on fire, so you had to be careful. There's an art to doing this right, because if you put too many chunks of coal in the furnace, the fire will smother itself—then you have an even worse job on your hand the next day. All the coal would have to be removed by hand and you'd have to start all over again. If you didn't put in enough coal, the fire would burn itself out by about four or five a.m. and you'd wake up to a cold house. If you did it right, there would be enough glowing coals when you woke up to easily start the fire again just by piling some more lumps of coal on top of the embers. What a daily adventure today's generation of kids have missed out on since the advent of gas furnaces!

I remember one cold winter morning, I over slept and the fire went out. To get it started again, I crunched up some old newspapers and piled some kindling on top, with some larger pieces of wood and a few chunks of coal placed on the very top. You usually had to wait until the wood was burning well before you topped it off with some more coal, which would then eventually catch on fire. That day, it was very cold outside, probably -20°F, at least. I didn't want to stand around shivering for half an hour before the fire really got going.

I had seen my dad quick start the fire on occasion with a shot of gasoline. This seemed like a good time to try it. He always kept a gallon or two in the basement for cleaning purposes. Everything was ready, so I poured a cupful of gasoline over the paper and kindling, stood back a few feet, and threw in a lighted wooden match. Poof went the fire. Flames shot out almost to my face! The flames singed my eyebrows! I think that I had maybe added a bit too much gasoline. The fire was really going, though, and in no time flat, I was able to add some more coal and retreat to my warm bed.

When I went upstairs, there was quite a distinct smell of gasoline in the house. "What's that smell, Duane?" inquired my mom. "It smells like gasoline to me. You didn't use it to start the fire, did you? You know that you could burn the house down if you're not careful."

I had been caught red-handed, and there was no sense denying it. "I just used a little bit of gasoline, just like Dad showed me, Mom, honest" was my only defence. Within a few minutes, the house was warm, but I had learned my lesson to go easy on the gasoline next time I used it to start a fire in the furnace.

HOCKEY GAMES

During the winter, life revolved around the local hockey rinks in the Pass. As boys, we went skating at night, had hockey practices, or played hockey games. In between, we played shinny hockey on ponds, which we shovelled clear of snow, or played road hockey on the streets. After a Chinook wind, sometimes, we skated on the ice-covered roads, even though this was hardly good for skate blades. Life without hockey was unheard of, and there was a tremendous hockey rivalry between all the towns in the Crowsnest Pass, which intensified at the more senior levels.

Most kids could name just about every player on each team in the National Hockey League of which were the original six: Montreal, Toronto, Boston, Chicago, New York, and Detroit. I rarely missed a Saturday night National Hockey League game on television and revelled in Foster Hewitt's commentary about the games, a Canadian radio broadcaster most famous for his play-by-play calls for *Hockey Night in Canada*. Boys were intensely loyal to their favourite team, and fights would break out over unkind works about opposing teams or players.

The rinks in the Crowsnest Pass were anything but palatial. They smelled of ammonia in the dressing rooms, and stale cigar and cigarette smoke in the lobbies. This was long before smoking was banned in public places. The lineups for games were often crushing, and it was standing room for many games in unheated buildings, where you could always see your breath and had to wear gloves so your fingers didn't freeze.

For most minor hockey games, the ice wasn't cleaned between periods, only once the hockey game was over if then. By the third period, the players would be pushing a lot of snow. For senior hockey games, the local rink rats would line up, side by side, and hand sweep the ice between periods with push brooms. For playoff games, the ice would be flooded between periods with a steel barrel of water on wheels, which fed water through a pipe to a plank wrapped with burlap sacks. Only after all the games were over for the day was the ice flooded with a large hose, so that it would freeze solid for the next day. There was no heat inside the arena proper. Nobody had ever seen a Zamboni except on television.

The Bellevue Arena was located just to the south of Main Street and no longer exists, having been torn down many years ago and replaced with what is now a playground. Sometimes, the dressing rooms in the Bellevue Arena would be so cold that the water would freeze solid in the toilets. It was normal to be able to see your breath when you dressed for practices or hockey games. It was rare if your feet didn't freeze between periods. There is nothing more painful than frozen feet, and many a young hockey player would have tears in their eyes while they tried to thaw them out. The pain could be excruciating.

None of these hardships detracted from practices or games because we didn't know any better. We thought that these conditions were normal and took them for granted.

I always packed all my hockey gear over my shoulder to the arena in Bellevue, and so did practically every other boy I knew. I don't recall ever getting a ride to the rink. Very few parents ever watched the games, probably because they were worn out after working in the mines all day or working an afternoon or night shift. It didn't matter. For the minor hockey games, there was always an enthusiastic crowd of schoolmates and a few vocal mothers of some of the players.

I only remember having a few hockey pucks during my minor hockey days. One of them wasn't regulation size; it was about a quarter over size with large nicks off the edges, which made it hard to shoot and it was hard to raise it off the ice. You didn't dare loose a puck because you needed all you could lay your hands on for practices. When the practices were over, everyone would retrieve their own puck. Somehow, we managed to keep them straight.

Hockey sticks cost about $5 in the 1950s, close to a day's wage for an adult. This was a lot of money in those days. They were as precious as gold. Hardly anybody had an extra stick. I didn't know that failure to drop a broken stick was a penalty until I got called for taking one to the bench at a game in Fernie, BC. I intended to take it home and glue it back together. Most of the sticks felt like a piece of lumber and were as solid as oak. I swear that they were meant to last a lifetime.

Practically everybody wore used hockey equipment of every colour imaginable. There were no stores in the Pass that carried any equipment, so it had to be ordered from Sears or Eaton's catalogues. The one and only piece of new equipment that I ever owned was a pair of red hockey pants. My gloves had holes in the palms that were the size of pancakes. My hockey socks had so many patches, it was hard to see the original fabric. We used quart sealer rubbers to hold them up. Sock tape was unheard of.

While there was a lot of false bravado, fights were quite rare in minor hockey games. In senior games, however, the play seemed to revolve around fights. The only fight I ever had was in a home game in Bellevue, against our archrivals from Blairmore. Late in the third period, one of their better players, a ringer from Cowley, a small farm town to the east of the Pass, took a run at me behind the net. I got the best of him and sent him to the ice with a good body check. When he got up, his gloves were off and he wanted to go. Normally, I would have laughed it off, but I was in my hometown, and I guess that my reputation was at stake. I drifted him a good one right in his kisser, and he dropped to the ice. Before I knew it, Eddy Kemp, my coach, who was refereeing the game, had wrapped his arms around me to restrain me from hitting the opposing player again. A league referee hadn't showed, so the home coach had to referee the game. Mr. Kemp had a tight grip on me, and I could hardly move. The next thing I knew, my opponent had gained his feet and had started to swing at me. I danced around with my coach still holding on tight until some other players wrestled the other guy to the ground. He wasn't too happy with blood all over his face and sweater. I learned that there are no winners in most hockey fights because I had a deep gash in my knuckle. I had to wait until the next day to get it stitched together in Blairmore because there were no doctors in Bellevue at the time. After getting a stern lecture from the doctor on the evils of fistfights, I stayed out of trouble for the rest of my minor hockey career.

The key intermediate and senior hockey team in the Pass during the 1950s was the Coleman Grands. The Grands always played entertaining hockey to good crowds and had a strong fan base. They played in various leagues in the 1940s and 1950s. In the 1950s, handsome winger Fred Churla was one of the star players, who later had a tryout with the Calgary Stampeders senior hockey team. He grew up in a home beside my grandparents' house in Bushtown. Dick Koentges, an old neighbour of mine in Bellevue, was a top forward while the handsome, chiselled Skip Gettman was one of the most feared players in the league. You didn't dare cross him or you'd pay for it. Skip was one of the most intense players in the league. A young Ron Koury was another talented player. I dated his raven-haired sister, Barbara, from Coleman, for a while after I left the

Pass and before we both started university in Calgary. Ted Kryczka and Paul Fillewich were also good players. Grit and toughness were their trademarks and fights were fairly common. The Grands won the Alberta Intermediate Championship in 1947, and then went on to win the 1946–47 Western Canada Intermediate Playoffs and the Edmonton Journal Trophy.

CHRISTMAS CELEBRATIONS

Christmas really was a festive time for most residents of the Pass. The mines would all but shut down for a few days, and the miners and their families would spend time together at home and at church.

Garry Grisak (L), Tony Stoklosa, and Duane Radford (R) at Christmas (note the tree in background), 1961 (Photo Credit: Dennis Amos).

Practically every home would have a natural Christmas tree; many of them were hand cut near the towns, but some would be bought commercially. There was no such thing as an artificial tree. People took a lot of pride in decorating their trees with Christmas lights and bulbs. The sparkler bulbs (i.e., bubblers) were probably the most popular. It was common to wrap the trees with a long string of tinsel, usually silver, as a final decorating touch. The tree would often be put in a pail with some water, which had to be maintained so they didn't dry out too much. While people were concerned they might catch on fire, I don't remember this ever happening. Hardly anybody put lights outside on their homes.

Leading up to Christmas Day, and the exchange of gifts, children used to spend a lot time pouring over the Eaton's and Sears Christmas catalogues, the latter referred to as "The Sears Wish Book." The kids would often fight over these catalogues that featured toys and other holiday-related merchandise. We'd put markers on all the pages that had toys we wanted for Christmas. The ones in our house were ragged by the time the big day rolled around. I'm sure we drove our mother nuts. For a small-town kid like me that didn't have an opportunity to shop at these stores in a nearby city like Lethbridge or Calgary, it was the next best thing to being there. I think that most every family in the Pass cherished these catalogues and all hopes and dreams they represented.

We'd often go to my grandparents on Christmas Eve to celebrate their Polish customs. In Poland, people fasted on Christmas Eve, with a meatless supper served at the appearance of the first star, later in the day. Afterwards, we'd return to our house, where my parents would usually leave some Japanese (Mandarin) oranges, a few shortbread cookies, and a bottle of Coke for Santa on a kid's play table on Christmas Eve. The food would always be gone and the Coke bottle empty on Christmas morning. For some reason, I always remember the oranges being sweeter when I was a child than they are nowadays. I never could quite figure out how Santa got down our chimney, so my mother told he came in one of the doors.

Christmas Day celebrations included a turkey dinner with dressing, homemade cranberry sauce and pickled beets, mashed potatoes, carrots and peas, gravy, pan buns, homemade cucumber pickles, and homemade pastries, such as Christmas cake and shortbreads. Christmas dinner was served on Christmas Day. I don't remember ever drinking wine with Christmas dinner when we lived in the Pass, although wine is common nowadays. It wasn't until I reached my late teens that sweet, sparkling wines, like the Baby Duck brand, became Canadian favourites. A traditional Christmas dinner was held at our grandparents' or a relative's home, such as Aunt Alice and Uncle Slim Williams, in Coleman, or Uncle Fred and Aunt Margaret Radford, in Blairmore, or at our house.

Orville and Elaine May, Dennis Amos, Mary Jane Koury, Art and Beverley Carnahan, Duane and Adrienne Radford, Ted Amos (L–R), 1966 (Photo Credit: Dennis Amos).

On Boxing Day, many of the English families in our neighbourhood would have open houses. I'd always visit Ted and Sally Amos and often the Jim and Zena Svoboda household. Folks would drop by our house to exchange Christmas greeting and enjoy some good fellowship. Bobby Beck and Dange Ellison were two fun-loving visitors. Crown Royal rye whiskey was one of the most popular drinks at this time of year, mixed with Canada Dry; Demerara rum with

Coke would be a close second. Wine was practically unheard of at the time.

My dad could play the piano by ear and knew a lot of popular songs, so he'd usually strike up some entertainment for the guests during these drop-in events. Some of the local women belonged to church choirs and would join in the singing. At the time, there really was a strong sense of community in the Pass, something which has been lost along the way in most places in Alberta over the years.

Back then, it was illegal to sell lottery tickets in Canada, but that did nothing to dissuade locals from buying Irish Hospital Sweepstake tickets, which usually became available shortly before Christmas. The "Irish Sweeps" were illegal outside of Ireland. An inevitable topic of conservation during the Boxing Day celebrations at our home were hushed conversations about winning the Sweeps. Most people were so hard up, I'm sure just thinking about the prize would make them cry. To my knowledge, nobody from the Pass ever cashed in with prize money from the Irish Sweeps. I wasn't the only one who wondered whether all the Canadian sales ever left the country.

Almost without fail, the first major snowstorm of the year would arrive in the Pass between Christmas and New Year's Day accompanied by falling temperatures invariably down to about -20°F. Usually about two feet of fresh snow would fall during the storm, and it would often drift, blocking most of the roads in town.

COAL SHOVELLING WOES

Today's kids don't know how lucky they are or how soft their lives are compared to what it was like when I grew up in Bellevue, where coal fuelled furnaces and you couldn't just turn up a thermostat to heat your house.

On New Year's Day in 1962, my dad said, "Okay, boys, she's all yours. Let me know when you're finished, and we'll take the truck back to the garage." I was sixteen years old. My brother, Jimmy, and

I grudgingly went to work. Rhythmically, we scooped shovel after shovel into the coal bin beside our garage. Each shovel was one less until the box was empty. The banjo shovels dug deep into the coal. Have you ever emptied a coal truck one shovel at a time? There were literally tons of coal—actually over five tons in this case—to be shovelled out of the box in the truck. That's right—over 10,000 pounds of coal. Few words were spoken between us. The only thing that kept me going was the sure-fire knowledge that there would be an end. Why didn't my dad buy a house where you could dump the coal down a coal chute, like many of the other homes in the Crowsnest Pass?

You'd think that being a trucker, my dad would have designed a bin where you could dump the coal right into it. Those were the jobs I liked best: drive up to the house, talk to the woman of the house, back right up to the coal room, set up a chute, and lift the box of the truck using a hydraulic hoist. Gravity did the rest of the work, spilling the contents into the chute, although there would be a few shovels of spilled coal to heave into the coal bin once the load was dumped. After the dust settled, you handed over the bill and hoped you would get paid. Not that everyone did pay up because unemployment was high in the Crowsnest Pass—on the Alberta side—and money was scarce in the 1960s, much like in the 1950s. Later, when my dad's trucking business went bankrupt, my mother told me that my dad had many outstanding bills because lots of folks just couldn't afford to pay for the coal orders.

Thank God for my brother, Jimmy. He was two years older than me and not the type to ever complain about hard work. In a way, he was an inspiration! If he could do it, so could I. This wasn't like a summer day, though, when I usually helped Jimmy, or my dad, unload a coal truck. Then and there, I made up my mind that I was going to better myself and go to university and I was going to get a good job! No truck driving or jobs in coal mines for me, with the ever-present danger of cave-ins and methane explosions!

Who wouldn't worry about their own safety considering all the disasters that had happened in the past century in the Crowsnest Pass? The Pass had a long history of natural disasters: floods, landslides, and fires. It is famous for the Frank Slide in 1903, when a ninety-million-ton wall of limestone split from Turtle Mountain, burying at least 70 men and women in the community of Frank. Mine explosions had killed over 300 people. Most of the low-lying areas in the towns had been ravaged by floods. The town of Fernie on the British Columbia side of the Crowsnest Pass had burned down twice. Winds of hurricane force had twice toppled buildings, blown out windows, and torn off roofs on the Alberta side of the Crowsnest Pass.

Back to the load of coal. On top of it being New Year's Day, it was -20°F, with a foot of new snow on the ground. That's about -30°C in today's terms, which is pretty darn cold. While my folks entertained some New Year's Day guests inside our home, my brother and I worked outside in the cold. My dad said he had done his part just getting the load of coal. How he did that on this first day of the year—a holiday, when everything was shut down—is still a mystery to me. As a truck driver, he no doubt had connections and could find a way to get a load of coal on any day of the year. Now, it was up to me and Jimmy to unload the truck. With few spoken words, we finally finished the job a couple of hours later.

It was on days like this that I could understand why Pa liked a couple of beers at the Bellevue Legion after a day's hard work. You could work up a thirst even when it was -20°F. Why did we have to run out of coal on New Year's Day, though? This was the sort of thing that made men out of boys. As the cliché goes, what doesn't kill you makes you stronger. My dad did the right thing. He worked his butt off all year long. New Year's Day was one of the few breaks for him.

"That's it," said Jimmy. "Let's go and get Pa." Finally, the truck was empty. Another day, another dollar—except on this day there would be no pay. Dad didn't pay us for shovelling coal into our own house. If it had been another home, that was different. Then we would be paid for the cost of the coal and hauling costs. He would give us a wage of $5 for a day's work. For a young boy, $5 a day was a windfall in the 1950s. Pa's hired help weren't paid much more, and he expected us to work every bit as hard as they did.

Don't let anyone try to fool you that shovelling coal when it is cold outside will keep you warm because it won't—at least not when it's -20°F with a north wind blowing. You may work up a bit of a sweat, but don't count on being very warm!

What a sight for sore eyes we were when the job was finally over—only a face that a mother could love, covered in coal dust as we were. No wonder that all the miners looked like racoons with black rings around their eyes. There was no possible way to ever get rid of it completely. We were one of the few families I knew of in Bellevue that had a shower. Some had bathtubs, but most heated water on a coal stove and poured it into a large tub for Friday or Saturday night baths. Our shower was in the unheated basement, save for what little heat the coal furnace pipes gave off, but it was a blessing to get cleaned up after the morning's work. After a few minutes, I felt like a human being again and ready to enjoy what was left of New Year Day. This was a watershed event in my life, as I vowed to go to university and did.

My dad's business folded after the coal mines shut down in 1962, and within a short time, he went broke. We had to sell our house. He practically gave away the transfer company assets, and the family moved to Calgary when I was seventeen, where I finished high school. It was a sad day to leave the Pass, but maybe one of the best things that ever happened to me.

5

TEENAGE YEARS

THE SAWED-OFF RIFLE

I've always been fascinated by guns, in particular handguns. Maybe I got this yearning from watching old television shows like *The Untouchables* and *Naked City*. Anyway, my dad picked up what we used to call a "rabbit gun" in his travels and gave it to me to supplement another .22 caliber rifle I was fond of borrowing from him. This "rabbit gun" was something else. I think it was used by trappers to finish off fur bearers because it had a short barrel, which was probably illegal even in those days. I couldn't hit a thing with it, but it made a hell of a noise when it was fired because of the short barrel.

One thing led to another, and I had an idea that this would make a great handgun if I just cut off a bit more of the barrel and trimmed the butt off the stock. My dad had a great tool shop and all the tools I needed for the job. The first thing I did was cut off the barrel with a hacksaw. It had no front sight, but that didn't bother me. Then I cut off the stock just behind the pistol grip. Now, I had a nice, compact sawed-off rifle, just like the kind the sawed-off guns that gangsters and old-fashioned bank robbers used in movies of the day—totally illegal and I knew it. So, I did everything possible to conceal the gun and I never told a soul about it. I was pretty sure you would go to jail for a long time if the authorities ever caught you with a gun like this. Possession of what were termed "concealed weapons," like this sawed-off rifle, was probably a criminal offence.

Whenever I took it out of the house, I was very careful to hide it, and I had a good hiding place where I was sure nobody would ever find it—inside a false wall in the basement. I was living the dream. I would take the gun into the bush across the Crowsnest River, on the south side of our house, and pretend I was somebody important, shooting it at various and assorted targets. If it was loud as a "rabbit gun," it was twice as loud as a sawed-off rifle. It's actually a wonder the gun never blew up on me, but I could fantasize all I wanted when I had it afield.

I painted the stock a cream colour from an old can of paint I found in the basement and the barrel black. It really looked like a professional hit-man job. I was working on the idea of making a holster for the gun one day when the town policeman drove up to my house. Mr. White was a pretty good guy. He had chubby cheeks, an easy smile, and wasn't cruel like most cops were in those days. If you were going to have a run in with the town cop, this was the best guy I had run across. I knew I was in trouble right away when Mr. White said, "Duane, I think you know why I'm here, don't you?" My goose was cooked and this was it. I stammered that I didn't know what he was talking about and didn't think that I hadn't done anything wrong. "Come on, Duane. Don't make it any harder on yourself and I'll give you a break. You know I'm here after the sawed-off rifle. Now, where is it?" he asked.

I don't think that I could have possibly felt any worse or guiltier! There was a police car parked in my front yard, and I was sure all the neighbours were watching. This was a big embarrassment back in those days in small-town Alberta, where everybody knew everybody's business. It looked like the town cop was on the verge of arresting me. I'd probably end up in a home for juvenile delinquents and never see my folks again. The words "juvenile delinquent" hit home—those were bad kids, always in trouble with the law. What was I going to say? He obviously had some inside information and knew about the sawed-off rifle.

"I've got all day, or maybe you'd like to come down to the police station and we can talk about this a bit more," he said. Mr. White really knew how to scare a kid. What harm was the sawed-off rifle anyway? I was only using it to play with, but I was trapped and I knew it. It looked like it was either come clean or else go to jail. I had thoughts of appearing in court and getting a whooping fine I wouldn't be able to pay. I had heard about jails and what could happen to young kids in them.

I broke down and confessed. I said that I would get him the sawed-off rifle but that I didn't know there was anything wrong with having one. I thought that it would be best to play dumb and hope for the best under the circumstances. All the while, I was wondering who would have ratted on me and how the cop knew that I was at home working in the garage at the time. Was it a neighbour, one of my friends, or my parents? I would never find out.

I retrieved the rifle from its hiding place and gave it to the town cop. "This is just between us, Duane," he said. "Now, what are we going to do with this illegal gun?" What could I say? He looked around the basement and spotted a heavy-duty steel vise on a nearby post. Without saying anything, he put the end of the barrel in the vise and tightened the grip. Then he pulled on the stock until the barrel was bent and took it out again. There was no way I was ever going to use the sawed-off rifle again with a twisted barrel. That done, he said that I hoped I had learned a lesson and that he wouldn't have to come by again. He left with the bent and twisted sawed-off rifle, shattering my dreams.

I was mad. I was heartbroken. The sawed-off rifle—my pride and joy—was wrecked. I guess that I was also relieved; at least, I wasn't going to jail or to reform school for juvenile delinquents. I could have cried but for my pride being hurt. I never did find out who tattled on me, but suspect it was an inside job. Regardless, I learned something about being responsible and to respect police officials, who often have a difficult and thankless job.

IN THE GOLD CREEK VALLEY AND BEYOND

Most boys in the Pass grew up with a .22 calibre rifle in one hand and a fishing rod of some sort in the other hand. The .22 calibre rifles were used for gopher shooting, plinking and bagging "chicken" (i.e., grouse), and featured inexpensive ammunition. Hiking in the nearby outdoors was a rite of passage.

I spent many a happy day hiking, hunting, and fishing in the Gold Creek Valley, north of Bellevue. Some days, I went alone, but usually I travelled with an old friend, Blythe Mattson, who was always easy to get along with and a great companion. One of Blythe's virtues was not being an early riser, and whenever I knocked on his door in the dark of the morning, his mother, Huberte, would invariably answer and invite me in. No, Blythe wasn't up yet, but she was working on him. "Dynamite, get up! Your hunting partner is here," she used to shout. ("Dynamite" was a nickname Blythe's mom called him. His friends called him by another nickname—Popeye—don't ask me why.) Blythe would appear sleepy eyed from his room! Huberte always fed Blythe a good breakfast of fried eggs and toast before we were off and gave me a cup of steaming coffee while we waited. I had already eaten before I arrived, but she always asked me nonetheless if wanted some fried eggs and toast.

We knew about game hunting laws and season dates, but I'm not sure that they were always strictly adhered to because fresh meat was at a premium at most homes in the Pass. In the autumn, we were after grouse, which were a welcome addition to our diet. The valley had its share of blue grouse, spruce grouse, and ruffed grouse. Locals called the spruce grouse "fool hens" because they were usually as dumb as a sack of hammers and rarely flew away. If you saw a "fool hen," it was as good as dead. The ruffed grouse and blue grouse were a different matter and were wary as all get out. The secret was to try to take the mother grouse out of action before she took off with her family or scattered the flock.

We used to hunt these birds with .22 calibre rifles and tried to shoot them in the head; it was not considered sporting to shoot them in the body. Now, if you haven't done it, hitting a grouse in the head is no easy matter, as they bob around like a boxer. If you aim at the base of their neck and carefully time your shot you can usually get them on the first shot. We used to practise all summer by hunting gophers, and we were pretty good shots.

There were several abandoned mine buildings in the Gold Creek Valley, and we would often explore them on our hikes. One day, we went into a place that local miners called the "hoist" to see what we could find. No sooner had we entered the building than we saw a bunch of pack rats scurrying about. These rodents could easily climb up cement walls and go across the ceilings. They had nests behind cupboards and in the corners of the buildings. We used to shoot them whenever we got a chance because everybody hated rats in those days. There must have been a family of pack rats in this particular building because they seemed to be everywhere. Blythe and I started shooting, and before we knew it, there were dead rats all over. I could see one in the far corner, peeking out from behind a cupboard, and I carefully lined up for a shot. It was probably about forty feet away. After the crack of the rifle, I felt something hit my chest. Looking down, a rifle bullet lay at my feet. It had ricocheted off the corner wall and fortunately was more or less spent when it hit me. I never fired in a mine building again, which on reflection was a stupid thing to do.

Another time, Blythe and I holed up in an abandoned trapper's cabin near a place called the "corrals" to wait out a rainstorm. It was dry in the cabin. Being a bit wet, we decided to light a fire in the air-tight stove to dry off before we continued with our trip. Before long, we had a good fire going and were soon dry as toast. I didn't think that we had too much wood in the stove when we left, although a small fire was still burning. We had a good day hunting grouse. Both of us had bagged several ruffed grouse, even though I don't think we had a hunting licence. The grouse were stuffed in our packs for the trip home.

As we rounded a corner on the trail, we encountered a forest ranger, who was manning a water pump connected to a fire hose. In those days, forest rangers were responsible for enforcing the game act. Our hearts were beating pretty fast, because if he checked our packs, we knew that we were in deep trouble. We could lose our rifles and maybe even go to jail. Luckily, the ranger didn't say a word. A little further down the trail, there were more forest rangers and some fire trucks. We decided that enough was enough and hit the bush before they saw us. There was no way we were going to risk being checked. It turned out that they were in the process of putting out a forest fire, which started near the abandoned trapper's cabin where we had been earlier that morning. We never knew for sure how the fire got started but had our suspicions.

There were days when Blythe and I thought that we could perhaps cover a bit more ground if we had some transportation, like a horse. We knew that some of the locals pastured their horses in a field above the old ball diamond, in the Dairy area. Early one Saturday morning, we decided to see what kind of horses were around and maybe take one for a test drive—at least until we gained some elevation, when we could turn it loose.

I always hated the first mile of the trail, as it was all uphill and rocky at that. As luck would have it, there was a good-natured sorrel horse in the pasture that seemed quite friendly and accommodating. I was not a horseman, and I don't think that Blythe was much ahead of me. Anyway, the horse had a halter, so we decided to try our hand at "rustling," which was against the law. We didn't really consider this to be "rustling" in a strict sense because we had every intention of returning the horse at the end of day. It looked like it needed some exercise anyhow. We got the sorrel horse positioned beside a big rock so that Blythe could get on it—no small feat without a saddle and stirrups—while I held a halter rope. All was going well.

Next, it was my turn. Up I went—but not before I passed Blythe our two .22 caliber rifles. This was going to be okay, I thought. The horse didn't seem to mind having two riders. Blythe said, "Giddy up," or something like that, and off we went toward the gate, at a gentle lope. We hadn't gone very far before the horse had enough of the piggyback riders—it was rodeo time. The horse bucked a few times before I got thrown off first, and within seconds, Blythe was also airborne. Thanks goodness for the nimble bodies of the young! We both survived the fall. Sadly, the stock of my rifle was not so lucky; it was broken in two. That ended our horse "rustling" days, and we were back on shanks mare again. It was a lesson hard learned because the gun stock was damaged beyond repair and had to be replaced.

One day, we really had a lot of energy and decided to hike eastward over top of the Livingstone Range into the Rock Creek drainage and do some serious gopher shooting. This was a tough hike because you had to cross over the mountains and descend into the foothills, and then repeat the process to get home. It was about nine a.m. when we were over the mountain range and down in the valley bottom near the headwaters of Rock Creek.

We had heard about a deranged man who lived in the area and had threatened crews working on the Trans Mountain Pipeline with trespassing on his property. Apparently, he was a squatter and had no property rights. The RCMP had apprehended this squatter after he had damaged some heavy construction equipment, so we felt it was safe to wander around the area. Before long, we stumbled across what had to be his home, which looked like it had been vacant for some time. I think he had been committed to an asylum near Ponoka. We called this place the "nut house." The door was closed but not locked. A couple of the windows had been broken or were knocked out.

There is a strange feeling when you enter a place like this: you know, deep down, you have no business being there, but your curiosity is just too great to stay out. The cabin must have been left more or less the same way as when he had lived in it before his misadventure with the law. At the time, this was a remote area, and it's quite likely nobody had been here since the police took him away. There were dishes in the sink, and food was still on the table. The wood box was half full, and there was an unmade bed in the corner of the kitchen. The place really had an eerie feeling about it, making my skin crawl. Off to one side, near the stove, was a storage room. Blythe and I gingerly looked around and made our way into the kitchen area. We had gone past the stove and woodpile when suddenly a skunk with a bunch of little ones came out from behind the wood box. We were trapped!

The family of skunks was between us and the door. The only way out was through a broken window in the far corner of the room. The mother skunk had her tail in the air and was prancing around and stomping her feet. This was a signal she was getting ready to do her business on us. I thought that we were goners. The little ones weren't sure what was going on and darted in all directions. I just couldn't imagine hiking more than ten miles back home, over the top of the Livingstone Range, all the while stinking of skunk scent; the thought was too much to bear. It didn't take me long to get my leg out and over the window sill and onto a ledge on the edge of cabin. There was a bit of drop, but it was the lesser threat of the other alternative. Without hesitation, I jumped to the ground, rifle in hand. Blythe was next. He had almost pushed me out in his frantic efforts to vacate the premises. He came out like he was bailing out of a bomber and hit the ground a running. We were breathing hard and laughing at the same time. How the family of skunks managed to get into the cabin is a mystery. Who would have ever expected a damn skunk to be living in a house with a closed door?

SUMMER JOBS

Teenagers had a tough time finding any kind of work at all in the Pass in the 1950s. There was virtually no part-time work for school kids. This was before the era of fast-food outlets, and people tended to eat at home. Even the full-grown men had a hard time finding steady work. Part-time work for teenagers was practically non-existent, except for the odd paper route.

I would work for my dad whenever he had any extra work, but this was spotty and often based on odd jobs that he got. During the summer, I'd help my dad collect garbage; he had a contract with the village. He'd drive one of his old coal trucks, and I'd pick up garbage barrels and tip them into the box of the truck. Often the garbage would reek of maggots. The odd time the bottom would fall off a barrel; I'd have to shovel the garbage into the truck. It was a filthy job. I'd also help my brother load coal ashes into one of my father's trucks.

Sometimes my dad hired me to help pump out septic tanks, which paid well. You could always tell something about the sex life in a family when pumping out these tanks. First off, you'd have to remove the lid from the tank to put in the suction hose before you primed the hand pump with a bucket of water on a disposal container on the truck. Catholics were not supposed to practise birth control, and these were in the time before birth control pills had been invented, so the rhythm method was in vogue, imperfect as it was. Many families used condoms regardless of church doctrines, and they'd be floating on top of the septic tank, in the dozens or hundreds in some cases. They'd plug the pump and had to be removed by hand so that it would work properly.

Being my dad's helper was something else. I can still remember the first time I ever drove one of his coal trucks, which also substituted as garbage trucks until he lost the town contract. Although I never really understood the implications of him loosing this contract,

I can remember the chill in the air when he told my mom about the bad news.

The first truck that I drove was a GMC that was rated to carry five tons, although it was often loaded with up to six tons. Anyway, we had dropped a load of garbage at the local dump and were on our way home for lunch. My dad said it was time I learned how to drive. This was before the days of AMA driver training for kids, obviously. "Why don't you drive home, Duane. You've got to learn sooner or later," he said.

I didn't have a learner's permit, never mind a driver's licence at thirteen years of age. My feet could reach the pedals, though. Plus, I had watched my dad and the hired man I usually worked with, Wilfred Wyatt, work the gears often enough that I was game to try it. I'm not sure I fully understood the purpose of the transfer case, but that is another story. Now, first gear is where it all starts, so I popped the clutch, and with a bit of a lurch, we were off. Next, shift to second gear and so on.

"Don't drive too fast, Duane. We're not in a road race," cautioned Pa. How many times was he to repeat those words over the years? That phrase, and "Rome wasn't built in a day," which came in a close second. "A little hard work never hurt anybody" was another favourite.

Before long, we were on the main highway; as I wound up the motor, I started to get just a little chicken. The steering wheel had so much play that driving the big truck was like herding cats down the road. I thought for sure that I would have a wreck and kill us all—or worse yet, go off Highway 3 and crash into the Frank Slide and be blown to smithereens. What a white-knuckle ride back to town and home, especially navigating around the bend into Bellevue, which was a trucker's graveyard because there was no slope to the curve and many a rig didn't make the turn. I wasn't the best at double-clutching and must have worn off a pound of gears as we slowed down coming into town, but Dad never complained. It was a proud cowboy who brought the truck into the front yard. Perhaps that explains why I passed my driver's test and chauffeur's test with flying colours when the time eventually came to be formally tested. Since there were no driving lessons in those days, you had to learn the hard way—by experience.

If my father didn't have any work for me, I'd take whatever jobs I could get, including maintenance of my grandfather Radford's gravesite in the Bellevue Union Cemetery. My aunts Beatrice Christie and Jessie Radford in Calgary would pay me a stipend for my time and effort, to keep the grass down and the fence around his gravesite freshly painted. He was crushed between two mine cars in the Bellevue Mine, having worked his whole life in the mines, starting when he was just eight years of age in England.

One summer, when things were desperate, Dennis Amos and I decided to hitch hike to the Burmis Lumber Company sawmill bush camp to see if there was any work. Lots of guys from Bellevue worked there, some full time and some just as a summer job. Dennis's brother Allan (Chuck) told me that he spent a few years there working with Dean Barlow, marking trees to be cut down and, on the landing, pulling cable (marking the logs to the best lengths they could get out of each log).

We didn't actually know where this camp was located, and neither of us had been anywhere in this part of the county. As it turned out, the mill was located on Lost Creek, a tributary of the Carbondale River. We weren't afraid of anything in those days. We told our parents where we were going and headed off towards Hillcrest. Hillcrest was the starting point of sorts for the Burmis Lumber Company, which operated three sawmills on Lost Creek. Before long an empty logging truck picked us up and asked us where we were going. We told him that we were headed for the Burmis sawmills to look for work and asked him if he was headed that way. As things turned out, the mill was his destination. The logging truck driver was a young man in his mid-twenties and as tough as nails.

He never said another word during the rest of the trip on our way to this sawmill.

It was a white-knuckle drive over the Adanac Summit. I didn't realize that trucks could go so fast. The ride brought back memories of tales my dad had told me about hauling coal from some strip mines on the Adanac Summit in the middle of winter and what a steep, treacherous, winding road it was. I held my breath most of the way. The dust on the gravel road was enough to choke a horse. Eventually, we rounded a corner and there it was.

I had seen movies of German concentration camps from World War II, and the sight brought back these memories. If there had been a Hollywood movie set for "Deliverance," this would have been it. What a sketchy sawmill! Try to imagine an old ghost town populated with shacks made of lumber, no paint, with mud and dirt everywhere. I recall that a small stream, Lost Creek, flowed under the workings of the working sawmill. There was a burner belching wood smoke and sparks. Skidders were hauling logs and kicking up dust. How could people live and work in a place like this? And yet they did, for months on end. I was terrified of the thought that Dennis and I might find some work here.

Anyhow, the truck driver told us where the head office was and said that he would give us a ride back to Hillcrest if we needed one. I didn't know what to do. Should I stay in the truck and have another hair-raising ride home, or take a chance on finding a job? I didn't have the foggiest idea where I was, and neither did Dennis. How would we ever get home again if we missed our ride? The thought was enough to spur us on. Dennis and I stood by the counter in the main office and meekly asked the mill foreman if they had any work for us boys—just temporary, mind you. What a relief when he said that they weren't hiring anyone in the next while. We were out of the office and on our way back to the haul road in a matter of seconds. The ride back wasn't quite as scary, because with a full load, the driver couldn't get up the same amount of speed. He didn't waste any time, though, and I was reminded of my dad telling me that these men were paid by the load. If they didn't work, they didn't get paid. They drove as fast as they could to get in as many loads as possible each day.

Dennis Amos and I could usually count on getting some work during the summer baling hay and building barbed wire fences for ranchers in the foothills near Lees Lake, to the east of Bellevue. Farmers paid up to $8 a day, which was a small fortune in those days. Mind you, they worked you hard from about eight a.m. until after supper; you earned your pay. By comparison, in 2018, the minimum wage in Alberta was $13 an hour, due to rise to $15 an hour, which is a huge difference. When I was a teenager, the hourly wage was $1 an hour. We were old enough to drive a car and would leave home early in the morning and head out for the local farms. I remember having the front tire blow out while turning a corner on a gravel road by Lees Lake, that being the first time I'd ever had such a misfortune. Luckily, there was a spare tire, but we lost our day's wages getting the tire repaired. Having a blow out on a gravel road in a vehicle without power steering is quite a challenge, as it is difficult to bring it under control and not roll over, so we were fortunate nobody was hurt.

One summer, an old school friend of mine from Blairmore, Melvin Williams, and I were haying for a rancher north of Lundbreck, who lived beside Connelly Creek. Melvin later made a career in the RCMP. The last time I saw him was at a highway check stop on Highway 2, near High River many years ago.

I was a strong kid for my age. I could work all day beside grown men, no doubt from the days I spent with my brother and dad hauling garbage and shovelling coal. We were told to work with the hired hand that was a man of few words. The owner of the ranch gave him a free hand over us boys, and he knew it. Funny, but he almost always seemed to drive the tractor. Melvin and I were either picking up or stacking bales on the hay wagon.

When a tractor is moving, there is no time for loitering and you have to walk along and pick up the bales and toss them onto the wagon; there is no stopping along the way. If you are in a low spot that has accumulated runoff, and thus increasing the yield of grass, the bales could weigh seventy to eighty pounds. On the level, most of the bales could weigh about thirty to forty pounds.

I would be on the ground because I was stronger than Melvin, and it was easier for him to stack the bales, but it was still hard work. The hired hand sat up front like King Tut and drove the tractor. He was the boss, so Melvin and I didn't complain. Things went okay for the first couple of days, but on the third day, Melvin was tuckered out and just couldn't pile the bales fast enough. If you don't stack the bales properly, they will fall off, which was what happened. We must have lost half the load on a sharp turn. The hired hand was livid and asked us what the hell we were doing back there. That was enough, and I exploded with a string of expletives. I told him, "You've been sitting up there on your fat ass for the past two days doing bugger all. Why don't you get off the tractor and help? If you don't like what we're doing, you can stick this job up your ass! And if you want to make something of it, just try me!" I had absolutely had it with him.

Melvin didn't say a word. The silence was deafening. You could hear the wind rustle in the grass. For a few moments, nothing happened. This was showdown time, and I was ready for a fight. "All right," said the hired man, "let me give you a hand." He got off the tractor and started loading bales. "Melvin, you take it easy for a while, and drive the tractor for a spell." When the wagon was loaded, we went about our work and never said another word about the spill. A line had been drawn and it was respected. The hired man did his share of work for the next few days until all the bales were stacked for the winter. At the end of the job, he thanked us and said we were more than welcome to come back at any time. I guess that I had made my point by taking a stand that he'd gone too far with his liberties.

THE ONE(S) THAT GOT AWAY

Fishing has always been a part of my life and just about all the kids I grew up with, although I didn't get off to an auspicious start as a fisherman. My aunt Alice took pity on me during a family picnic on Corbin Creek in British Columbia. "What's the matter, Duane? How come you're so sad?" she implored. I was five years old and without a fishing pole. All the other male members of the group had gone fishing. How was I to feel? My feelings were hurt and I decided to sulk. Secretly, I hoped they all fell in the river, or worse, for leaving me behind with the women folk. Some picnic—it hadn't got off to a good start. Aunt Alice said she would see what she could do, and low and behold, I'll be darned if she didn't find a willow pole with some fishing line that had a bright fly attached to it. I was in heaven. My very own fishing rod!

"Okay, Duane, let's go fishing," she said, as she took me down to the stream. I just knew I was going to catch something. Well, I tried and tried, but it was hard to cast the fly where I wanted it to land; it always seemed to get caught on some bushes or something. I was starting to get a little frustrated, but Aunt Alice always got the hook untangled and got me back in action. Then it happened. On one of my wicked back casts, I caught Aunt Alice in the cheek. Oh, oh . . . it didn't look good.

When she let out a howl, I knew my fishing was over for the day. I had lost my one and only fly, which was firmly stuck in her cheek. She started to cry, and then I felt even worse. I'm sure it hurt like hell. This just wasn't my day. We slowly walked back to camp for help. "I didn't mean to hook you, Aunt Alice, really. I'm very sorry" was all I could think of to say. This chatter seemed to help break the ice, and Aunt Alice kept repeating, "I knew I shouldn't have been so close to you. I was afraid this would happen."

We were in a real pickle because the nearest doctor's office was in Fernie, miles away, over rough mountain roads. In fact, I had wondered how my dad had made it in this far with his old car. When we got back to camp, my mother was waiting, relaxing beside the car—that is, until she saw her sister with blood all over her face. "What on earth has happened, Alice, are you all right?"

I'd never heard a woman curse before, but Aunt Alice made it very clear how she felt about the hook in her cheek. My mom cut the fishing line, so at least that nuisance was eliminated. Then she got out a first aid kit from the car and applied a dressing, cleaning up Alice's face as well. Now, the wait was on. Where were the men folk? They could be almost anywhere, and who knew when they'd return. It was a long time before my dad, brother, and my aunt's boyfriend at the time and future husband, Slim Williams, returned. Without any further ado, it was off to Fernie over a rough and bumpy road.

Aunt Alice hardly said a word. I didn't think it was a good idea to say too much either, even though I didn't mean to hook her. Later that evening, we finally arrived at the local doctor's office. By this time, my aunt's cheek was badly swollen and looked a lot worse for wear. I figured that I was in real trouble now. The doctor wiggled the hook around and finally had to push it all the way through her cheek so he could cut of the tip of the hook off and take it out. Three stitches later, and we were on our way home. Needless to say, we didn't keep the hook as a souvenir when the doctor asked if we wanted it as a keepsake.

Another time, I went fishing with my dad, Jimmy, and my uncle Carl Sapeta on Allison Creek, west of Coleman. It had been a good day, and I had taken some nice trout. About noon, I latched onto the biggest one I had caught all day—a whopper for a small stream! Wait until Dad saw this one; would he ever be proud of me! I fought the fish for what seemed like forever. Finally, he was played out and ready to land. It was too bad I was in a canyon with steep sides of loose shale. Not to worry, I'd just have to make the best of it. I could already taste this fat trout. Very carefully, I slid him up the shale slide and pounced on him. I had him! For a moment—then the slippery trout wiggled out of my hands and slid to the edge of the stream. I grabbed him again with both hands this time, hard. I didn't want to lose the biggest fish of the day. And then I slid down the steep shale bank into Allison Creek. In a wild effort to get some purchase on anything to arrest my slide, I let go of the fine cutthroat trout that rolled into the stream and darted away. I was too young to know very many swear words. It's probably just as well. The fishing trip was over for me—anything else would be anticlimactic!

Talk about swearing, one fine October day, Dennis Amos, his dad, Ted, and I were fishing on Daisy Creek, north of Coleman. The trout were really bunched up in their over-wintering pools. Trouble was, the stream was gin clear, and as soon as they saw you, they shied away. It was very frustrating; there were all these fish practically at your feet, and they wouldn't bite worth a darn. We had been fishing for hours and had only caught a few fish. After losing one of the few that I had enticed to bite, I was fit to be tied. I was really getting exasperated. On losing the fish, I let out a string of expletives that would have done justice to a sailor; at least, I had gotten that bad feeling off my chest. The fish had really gotten the best of me. "Tsk-tsk," said Ted, "that's no way to talk, is it, Duane? They're only fish, and you're supposed to be smarter than they are, aren't you?" Ted was always a real gentleman who showed good manners. He was right, and I hardly ever cursed when I lost a fish again. We were, after all, supposed to be smarter than them!

Not that I didn't have good reason to get really mad and swear on some other occasions. On another fishing trip on Rock Creek, Blythe Mattson and I were working our butts off trying to catch fish. The vegetation along Rock Creek was like a jungle and a nightmare to get through. We had been fishing all morning and had nothing to show for it. Around about noon, we came to the Rock Creek Falls, a real honey hole for fish. If the pool below the falls didn't produce, then nothing would—this was pay dirt.

Low and behold, I caught a veritable monster on my very first cast. The fish darted this way and that until I finally played him out. Blythe was downstream of me taking it all in. He was no doubt savouring the trout that we intended to cook in some tin foil for lunch. I figured he was done for, so I asked Blythe to grab the end of the line and pull him ashore. Bad mistake. Blythe grabbed the line and lost his balance. The next thing, I knew he stumbled and the fish slid off the hook—no lunch that day! That was it! I was through fishing for the day, but I didn't say a word. Ted had taught me a good lesson. Blythe mumbled, "I'm sorry, it was a real nice trout. It's too bad he fell off the line, eh?" What could I say? The fish was gone and there was no point complaining or rubbing it in. I would suffer in silence.

It's funny but I can clearly remember just about every fish that I have ever lost—and almost all of them were veritable monsters in my mind!

TEENAGE YEARS—PLAYING PRANKS

Because my brother was a couple of years older than I was, I seldom hung out with him, or my sister, who was six years younger than me. I used to hang out with some neighbourhood kids, most of whom lived nearby: Dennis Amos, Larry Svoboda, Johnny Ellison, Jim Jepson, and Larry Quintilio, as well as Blythe Mattson and Tony Stoklosa, who lived in the Dairy area north of Main Street. Our old friend and elementary school classmate Garry Grisak, who had moved to Calgary, would sometimes come back to town for the summer.

There wasn't a lot of entertainment for teenagers in Bellevue when I was a kid. There were no malls back in those days. This was long before the days of the world-wide web and the internet. None of my friends had a car, so unless we hitchhiked to Blairmore, we were stuck in Bellevue, which was not exactly the entertainment or cultural centre of the Pass. If we stayed in Bellevue, our entertainment would be loitering beside the Bellevue Café, watching cars go by. There was usually no way we would go to Coleman, which had a reputation as a rough town, and we didn't fancy getting beat up by the local thugs. You only went there during daylight hours, and only with a bunch of other boys. You didn't dare stay too long, or you would run the risk of getting beat up by the locals, especially if they thought you were after "their girls," which we were. For some reason, Coleman seemed to have more than its share of very attractive and mysterious girls, some of whom I dated: Linda Marconi and Barbara Koury, for example.

Halloween was always a big day in the Pass—in Bellevue in particular. Usually there was no snow on the ground. Kids would dress up in homemade costumes (generally hand-me-downs) but did not go out until it got dark. They'd shout, "Trick or treat," when they approached a house. If nobody answered, it was not uncommon for at least some kids to throw eggs on the house—in kid's parlance "egging it" as payback. Folks would sometimes gift toffee apples, candy pencils, candy, and popcorn balls. We knew the honey holes and would travel far and wide to get the best and most treats. Most kids used a pillow sack to collect their booty. There were lots of Halloween parties throughout the Pass.

"Gate Night" was the eve of Halloween, the night before the big day, and it was always the worst day of the year for pranks. The cops would often deputize men as "special constables" to help them patrol the streets to deter vandalism. Curfew bylaws would be enforced, and no one under the age of sixteen would be allowed on the streets after nine thirty p.m. On each Halloween and Gate Night, the local town police would send out stern warnings to the school kids that they would be patrolling all night long, and any vandals would be put in jail. Yes, jail!

Homeowners absolutely dreaded Gate Night, which came by its name honestly. This was the night when pranksters used to steal the gates on fences around their houses. Sometimes, garbage barrels would be set on fire or turned upside down. Tipping over outhouses was another prank. Very few homes had indoor plumbing in the 1950s, and outhouses were common in Bellevue. We used to scout out these outdoor toilets, weeks ahead of Gate Night, to make sure we knew where to find them when the big night finally arrived. Tipping over an outhouse is no small job and takes the efforts of several strong young men to do it properly, particularly if you don't want to get caught by the owner.

One of the biggest ones I had ever tipped over in the Dairy was so big it took five us to dislodge it—what a stunt that was. Your timing had to be perfect, or you would fall into the hole, which was full of you know what. This was no small job when it was dark either. When the neighbourhood dogs were all barking, you just knew it was just a matter of time before the homeowner was going to figure out what was happening and would likely shoot you with a load of buckshot. Seriously, this was a dangerous prank, and some kids were shot at, probably with salted loads, not pellets. I always hoped the shotgun would be loaded with rock salt, as I couldn't bear the thought of my mother picking shotgun pellets from my backside. I never got hit, but I got shot at a couple of times by a neighbour, a school teacher. Funny thing is, the local town cop never seemed to investigate these shootings.

On one particular Gate Night, my old friend Dennis Amos was locked up in the local jail by the town cop, Mr. Jones, for setting off fire crackers on Main Street. Jones said that Dennis and his buddies had to go back to jail on Halloween night. That didn't go over very well with Mrs. Gus Mattson, and after she told the cop off, Dennis and his friends were out for Halloween.

Another time on Halloween, Jim Jepson and some of his friends were standing around by the Royal Bank on Main Street, minding their own business, when the village constable decided they were the culprits that had pushed over someone's outhouse up the Dairy

Road (apparently no one was in it, and Jim said they had not). He hauled Jim and his friends over to the police station, where there was a jail cell and detained them for an hour or so, then told them to go straight home. Jim told me that his memory was a bit foggy on all the details, but his mum tore a strip off the cop that night or the next morning; she said he had no right to detain anyone without proof or charges. Jim didn't think that fellow lasted long in that job.

In a conversation between Tony Stoklosa and his long-time friend Allan (Chuck) Amos, they reminisced about the exciting events of Halloween and Gate Night. Tony said that many yards in town had removable fence gates, which vandals exchanged with neighbours or hung them in trees, and also recalled the activity of pushing over outdoor toilet structures.

One such caper—of which Tony did not participate in—involved his neighbour Tony Tuborski, a World War II veteran. He recalled it may have been the work of Tony's brother Stan, along with his buddies, Russel, George, and Billy MacIntyre. Somehow, Tuborski's outhouse was pushed over onto its door side. Unbeknownst to the vandals, Mr. Tuborski was inside at the time doing his thing. Tony's father heard the screams of "Help, help," so he came to the rescue and attempted to right the structure. He could not move it; it was too heavy, as most outhouses were constructed of timbers and heavy planks with sheet metal roofs to prevent upsets due to very heavy fall winds roaring through Bellevue. His father ran to the woodshed to fetch a crowbar and sledgehammer. With these, he proceeded to dismantle the bottom of the outhouse. He extracted Mr. Tuborski by his feet most carefully as not to allow him to drop into the poop pit.

There was a horseback gang the locals called the "Night Riders," who intimidated the younger kids, especially at Halloween and on Gate Night. Actually, they terrified all the townsfolk. Nobody was sure just who actually belonged to the Night Riders because they wore white pillow cases as masks. Also, nobody knew just how many members belonged to this gang of older boys either. There must have been at least half a dozen young guys, though. There were suspicions they might have been from Hillcrest or the Maple Leaf area in Bellevue, but nobody knew for sure. Some of my friends recalled them being dressed like members of the Ku Klux Klan.

There were many rumours about who belonged to the dreaded Night Riders, but no real proof. They were on horseback and never rode except at night, down the gravel streets and alleys, as only Highway 3 was paved at the time and the only concrete sidewalks were downtown. I only saw them a few times—shadowy figures on horseback, usually riding fast. They could pull over an outhouse lickety-split with their horses, and you always walked in fear of them catching you with their lariats—or worse, running you down with their horse. The cops were always on the lookout for the Night Riders but never made any arrests that I heard off. They were smart teenagers or young adults, good riders, and could avoid the police by heading for the hills at the first sign of danger. It was spooky to see them riding the streets of Bellevue at night, their horse's hooves kicking up gravel as they pounded the streets. My old neighbour Allan (Chuck) Amos said Jackie Evans told him his brother belonged to the Night Riders and said they were "just a bunch of kids raising a little hell." Chuck told me, "I have no idea who would know any more. I think anyone who might have known are all gone now." One Halloween, we decided to do something a bit different. We went to the local gas service station on Main Street and drained the hoses of gasoline into tin cans. In those days, the hoses never drained completely and usually had a small amount of gas in them. You could get half a quart or more of gas from most of them if you angled them towards the ground into a container. We would pour some of the gasoline in a line across the main highway that ran through town and wait for a car to approach. Just before it reached the line of gasoline, we would set it on fire. You can imagine the reaction of the driver as he hit the brakes to avoid the wall of fire. This was great fun, and the car would come to a screeching halt. I don't remember how many times we did this before the local cops came around. They were wise to us and were hiding behind the Royal Bank while we walked towards the Dairy area. The chase was on.

Now, the best thing to do in a situation like this is to split up. There were four of us and two of them. I headed south into a back alley as fast as my legs would carry me. Three of my friends got caught, but I was too fast. They later told my parents that they knew I was there but couldn't quite catch me. It's amazing how fast a person can run when they're being chased by the police—even if you're not in shape. My friends were the school heroes the next day, having spent the better part of the night in jail. Their parents had to come and bail them out at midnight.

Our foot speed really came in handy when we played Nicky Nicky Nine Doors. This somewhat twisted game was always played at night, usually after eight p.m., when it was dark. One brave boy would walk up to the front door of a house and knock on the door. Then he would take off and hide, usually around the side of the house. When the occupant opened the door, naturally nobody was there. The owner would close the door. This would be repeated, with the same result. After the second time, the gig was up the owner was ready to spring into action. As soon as the knocking started for the third time, he would bolt out of the house and try to catch the prankster. You really had to have a lot of nerve in these cases and be quick on your feet. This wasn't a game for chickens. If you got caught, at the very least, you were going to get your rear end kicked, big time. Worse, you could get beaten around the head a bit and sent home; most of the miners could pack quite a wallop. Sometimes, your parents would be called and told in no uncertain terms what was thought of your upbringing. So, you had to be fast. There were many times when I made a 100-yard dash in close to 10 seconds when a big man was hot on my heels. I could really make tracks when I was scared!

The same hazards applied when we went raiding gardens during the summer. We would crawl over the fence into some of the better gardens in town and steal the best vegetables. It wasn't very often that the owner even knew what was happening, but just about everybody in town had a dog that would bark like crazy when someone came into their backyard. That was enough to tip people off, and they would come outside to investigate. Our neighbour Kas Farfus really took exception to us raiding his garden that was always one of the best in town. He must have slept by his back door, waiting for us to try something. And could Kas ever run. Whenever we raided his garden, we always posted some lookouts and were especially careful. He was almost as fast on his feet as us kids; fortunately, he never caught us, and I don't think he ever figured out who we were.

JUNIOR AND SENIOR HIGH SCHOOL

I attended three different schools during my junior and senior high school years, Grade 7 in Hillcrest, Grade 8 in Maple Leaf (in Bellevue), and Grade 9–11 in Blairmore from 1958–1963.

I had the following junior and senior high school teachers at Hillcrest, Maple Leaf, and Blairmore: Reno Bosetti, Keith Braithwaite, Louise Demchuck, Dave Halton, William Jallep, William Marcolin, Helen Muspratt, Eric Price, Joe Quintilio, Sam Richards, William Serra, and Frank Sickoff. And virtually all made a lasting impression on me as being stalwart teachers who could teach.

Hillcrest got its name from Hillcrest Mines and is located south of Bellevue. It's located just south and east of Turtle Mountain and the Frank Slide.

I took a school bus to Isabelle Sellon High School in Blairmore for Grades 9, 10, and 11. Isabelle Sellon High School was the first modern school I attended with a gymnasium, shower and change room, shop, and spacious classrooms. There always seemed to be a buzz in the air at this school, and I have many fond memories of attending classes there. I thought that most of the school teachers were very professional and highly committed as educators.

I was enrolled in a senior matriculation program during high school, so I would have the course material to get into university. When I took an aptitude test in high school to get some clues on what kind of occupation I might be suited for, the results indicated I was persuasive, so maybe I should have been in sales or real estate.

An old friend Peter Costigan and I were the only boys who took typing classes, which were full of girls. They were taught by Sam Richards, who also taught other subjects. (Peter married Marilyn Svoboda, a sister of my good friends Larry and Jimmy, who were close neighbours of ours.) If Mr. Richards got mad at a student, a mole on his forehead would inflame and turn purple. Mr. Richards would turn on an old record player. The students would type in keeping with the sound of the music, much like learning to play a piano in tune with the beats a metronome. We learned to type using the old-fashioned manual Underwood typewriters, where you'd have to throw the carriage to go to the next line. I got pretty good at typing possibly because I'd taken piano lesson until Grade 8, so I could find the right keys. At the end of my classes, I reached about forty-five words per minute, which was considered good for a typist back in the day.

School buses ran to and from school, rain or snow. I never heard of a "snow day," where we got to stay home. What a way to meet new girls! There was a different bunch every year. Also, the teachers never got a chance to get to know the students very well, so their reputations weren't common knowledge. Invariably, the school principals were tough—necessary, I think, to maintain discipline in school with a bunch of strong-willed young boys, and some girls, in class.

All students feared the strap. Even the toughest boys would break down after some of the sessions they endured. There were some big, tough kids in the Pass, but they were no equal to the even tougher principals, many of whom had spent time in the mines.

Thursday, *October 11, 1962*, The Lethbridge Herald, page 5.

AWARD RECIPIENTS—Presentation of academic awards to students took place recently in the Catholic Hall in Bellevue. Those receiving awards were:

Front row (L–R): #1 Lucille Dugdale, #2 Eileen Betts, #3 Linda Dambois, #4 Carol Kuban, #5 Marvis Truitt, #6 Belle Marcolin, and #7 Millie White.

2nd row (L–R): #1 Janice Truitt, #2 Janet Kristoff, #3 Kathleen Makin, #4 Kay White, #5 Doreen Griffith, #6 Adeline Filipuzzi, #7 Geraldine Bianchini, and #8 Judy Hill.

3rd row (L–R): #1 Tony Stoklosa, #2 Wentworth Bjarnason, #3 George Vink, #4 Dave Barnett, #5 Duane Radford, and #6 Stanley Petricia.

4th (back) row (L–R): #1 Billy Grigel, #2 Simon Sencz, #3 Lawrence Kryzanowski, #4 Lee Sickoff, #5 Allan Halton, #6 Allan Betts, and #7 Jim Jepson.

Donating the awards were the Bellevue-Hillcrest-Mohawk Home and School Assn, Union Cleaners, Dr. R. B. Burgman, Bellevue Waterworks, Hillcrest Hotel, Catholic Women's League, Zees Style Shop, merchants of Bellevue and Maple Leaf, Spic and Span Cleaners, E. and A. Brazzoni, Hillcrest Miners Club, Saratoga Processing, J. and

C. Brazzoni, Calgary Power and the Village of Bellevue. Photo by Vern Decoux, Herald Engraving. (Photo Credit: Vern Decoux, The Lethbridge Herald, *1962).*

I remember one boy who met his match in Grade 8. He never said much and was as tough as nails. I had never seen him cry; he was one of the toughest kids I ever met. The type of guy you wanted on your hockey team. He wouldn't back down from anyone. One day, he went too far with the school principal, who decided it was time to show him who was boss. His reputation for giving a hard strapping was known far and wide. Nobody had ever come out of his office without tears in their eyes. This in itself was generally enough to keep most of the students in line; never mind the fact that most parents would give their kids a good spanking when they found out they had been given the strap. Generally, one or two good whacks with the strap were all it would take to make a boy cry—believe me, the strap hurt like hell. But teenage boys have a lot of pride and don't like to be labelled as crybabies. Fortunately, I never ran into a principal who would strap someone just to make a point. But this student was to meet this sort of person on the day in question. The longer he held out, the harder became the strapping. It went on for a long time before he returned to class, in tears with bright red eyes. The principal would make an example of a student so that all the others in school would get the message and toe the line. Afterwards, everybody would behave and the message would be passed down to the younger students, which served to perpetuate the legacy.

There were a lot of house parties and school dances when I was growing up. Curfews were unheard of for the most part. We never got in any trouble at a house party or dance, and nobody used to drink liquor—hardly, anyhow. I can remember the parents of one of the neighbourhood boys, Cyril McDonald, used to make homemade dandelion and some red wine. We'd pilfer some of the wine, from time to time, but it was too sour for most of us. Usually, the only way to get alcohol was from bootleggers, who apparently charged an arm and a leg for beer and hard liquor. There were no recreational drugs in the Crowsnest Pass at the time. Marijuana was unheard of.

Many did their best to wear "duck tail" haircuts, imitating Elvis Presley. I would spend hours trying to get the part just right in the back of my hair, which was a tough job unless you had really long hair. A jar of dark green Wave gel was used to set the duck tail, and once set, it was almost like glue. A long handled rat-tail comb was fashionable for hairstyling, especially for girls, because you could hold the tail end of the comb in your mouth while you used your hands to style your hair. Even the notorious Pass winds wouldn't rustle your hair if you applied enough of the Wave gel. You weren't considered to be properly dressed unless you had a "trucker's wallet" in your hip pocket, with a rat-tail comb stuck in for good measure— then you were cool. Most of the teenage boys I hung out with would have died to wear a black leather jacket because they idolized James Dean, a Hollywood rebel and heartthrob of the period. Sadly, leather jackets were too expensive for most families and but a dream for school kids.

I think that lots of students were getting sick and tired of rules and regulations at school. Some kids were striking out against what they saw as unnecessary order. In their minds, perhaps they had been pushed too far. This was the start of the age of graffiti and of small acts of defiance, like letting air out of teacher's tires and getting even with the establishment and the teachers, in particular, on Halloween and Gate Night. It was very dumb, you bet, and juvenile. Once the seeds for change had been sown in the 1950s, acting out like this set the stage for the often turbulent 1960s. There's little doubt that the 1950s marked the start of an era of teenage rebellion.

This was an exciting time for kids, as it marked the era of rock 'n' roll, a genre of popular music that originated and evolved in the United States during the late 1940s and early 1950s. The sometimes raunchy music was popular with school kids. Adults didn't necessarily like the music and thought it might be a bad influence on children.

Elvis Presley was the teenage heartthrob and hero in the early fifties. There's also some truth to the saying that the 1950s was a "decade of innocence" that featured many solo singers and quartet harmony bands, who sang harmonious romantic, love songs.

Some other top solo singers of this genre would have been Canadian Paul Anka, Pat Boone, Patsy Cline, Connie Francis, Lorreta Lynn, Dean Martin, Ricky Nelson, and Roy Orbison—just to name a few. A few of the more popular "harmony" genre songs in the 1950s were "Catch a Falling Star," "Chain Gang," "Love Is a Many Splendored Thing," "Magic Moments," "Three Coins in the Fountain," and "She Loves You." These songs had harmony. You could probably understand all the words in these songs, and their lyrics weren't vulgar.

Back in the Good Ole Days by Allan (Chuck) Amos

Verse 1:
Jukebox, bobby socks, poodle skirts, and loafers
Beatle mops, boogie tops, Elvis waves, and Joker
Brylcreem, James Dean, Buddy Holly frames
All these things are what we loved
Back in the good ole days

Chorus:
In the good ole days, you could go to the store and didn't have to
     lock the door
We went out for a dollar and put a gallon in the ole Ford
There were no computers or iPods, just an ole black phone on
     the wall
But we all survived the good times and bad, and mostly we had us
     a ball

Verse 2:
Blue suede shoes, Motown blues, Bo Diddley, and Chuck Berry
Hot rod cars, monkey handle bars, CCR, and "Proud Mary"
Zoot suits, biker boots, the Fireballs "Torquay"
All these things were what we loved, back in the good ole days

Chorus:
In the good ole days, you could go to the store and didn't have to
    lock the door
We went out for a dollar and put a gallon in the ole Ford
There were no computers or iPods, just an ole black phone on
    the wall
But we all survived the good times and bad, and mostly we had us
    a ball

Verse 3:
Ducktails, Dicky Dale, a tune called "Pink Canary"
No acid rain, no climate change, or a carbon tax to pay
No greenhouse gas, no GST, no stuff you had to bury
All these things were what we loved, back in the good ole days

Chorus:
In the good ole days, you could go to the store and didn't have to
    lock the door
We went out for a dollar and put a gallon in the ole Ford
There were no computers or iPods, just an ole black phone on
    the wall
But we all survived the good times and bad, and mostly we had us
    a ball

New Year's Eve parties really were the social event of the year. Even the kids got into the act and had great house parties. There was no door crashing, which was unheard of in those days. At midnight, it was traditional to kiss your date and anyone else nearby that you admired. Yes, it was common for mistletoe be hung at Christmas too in Pass homes, and it would still be a feature at New Year's Eve parties. After the midnight celebrations, the men and boys went outside with their rifles and shotguns and fired shells into the air. It sounded like a small war for about half an hour. Then it was back into the house, or home. I can remember one News Year's Eve party at the Ellison household where Johnny had all manner of shotguns that we fired at midnight: 12, 16 and 410 gauges. It seemed like practically every household was engaged with the "fireworks." While there may have been a bylaw prohibiting the discharge of firearms inside municipalities, it was never enforced and nobody gave as much as a thought about laying a complaint.

When someone turned age sixteen, their horizons really expanded because they could get a driver's licence. Then it was off to Blairmore and Coleman in search of girls. The far pastures always seemed greener for the opposite sex. Friday or Saturday night dances in Blairmore were the norm, with live bands that could really get the crowd dancing. As at school dances, it was customary for all the girls to line up on one side of the dance hall and all the boys on the opposite side. After the dance, it was off to the local café for Chinese food, usually just a bowl of sticky rice with plum sauce, which is about all that we could afford.

On Saturday nights, our entertainment often involved cruising the streets in Blairmore in a car, looking for girls to pick up. We'd drive up one side of the main street and down the other until someone worked up enough nerve to ask some girls if they wanted to go for a ride. It was hard to break ice with girls from other towns in those days until you got to know a few of them! This was always dangerous business because the local boys often took exception to these raids on what they saw as "their" girls.

I got egged into a fistfight with Rick(y) Aschacher, over an old flame of mine, Kathy MacDonald, on a Sunday afternoon in Blairmore. Rick told me to get out of town and leave her alone;

maybe he wanted to be her boyfriend because I had the impression that she'd dropped me. Aschacher was a good-looking guy, with dark, wavy hair styled in a pompadour cut. He had a reputation as a tough guy. I didn't start the fight; he did. He called me out for dating Kathy. You couldn't back down from a taunt like this, or you would be dead meat. If you didn't stick up for yourself, everyone would pick on you. So, you fought, whether you wanted to or not. There was no turning the other cheek. Neither of us landed a knock-down punch; the fight ended in a draw. You didn't have to fight very often because in small towns the word spread fast if you weren't a chicken. If you didn't back down, the tough guys and bullies tended to give you some respect and would leave you alone. I must have made a point with the boys in Blairmore, as after that, I had some other girlfriends in Blairmore—Janice Reese, Sandra Rinke, and Eleanor Krolli—without any further incidents.

Blairmore was the hub of the Pass in the 1950s in terms of social activities. There were midnight madness movies in the local theatre. There were curling bonspiels that drew teams from all over southern Alberta. The Bunny Bonspiel, held at Easter, was probably the most well-known bonspiel, which dates back to 1947. Dances seemed to be held practically every weekend at the Elks Hall in Blairmore, usually with local live bands, some of which were very good. Chuck Amos said that Willy Sygutek played with a band called the Teenagers ; the Four S's would be the Settlas and their dad. The Teenagers was made up of Willy Sygutek on guitar, Teddy Pier on drums, Don Smaniotto on the trumpet, and Ron Sekina on the accordion. Chuck said that Phil Lethbridge also played at the Elks Hall.

The Grade 12 students for the graduating 1964 term were as follow (sadly, I'd moved to Calgary and didn't get to graduate with them): Catherine Beck, Geraldine Bianchini, Lucille Brazzoni, Diane Carpenter, Grace Chomokovski, Wendy Chrystal, Peter Costigan, Adeline Filipuzzi, Kenneth Garbier, Robert Giza, Brian Gresk,

Alan Halton, Judy Hill, Sandra Hurtak, Carol Ironmonger, Gloria Jallep, Richard Jillain, Richard Koinberg, Eleanor Krolli, Lawrence Kryzanowski, Carol Kuban, Katherine (Kathy) MacDonald, Joan Marcial, David Petrone, Larry Quintilio, Kenneth Roome, Elsie Sartoris, Kenneth Sefcik, Anthony (Tony) Stoklosa, Luigi Tamborini, Sandra Tiberg, Marvis Truitt, Clare Willoughby, and Marie Wojszel.

The original fast-food outlets like burger stands, along with a Kentucky Fried Chicken outlet, began business in Blairmore, which was the hub of a lot of entertainment activities. The main liquor store was also in Blairmore, and so were three bars, or beer parlors as they were called in those days. Most bars in Alberta at the time had two entrances: one for "Men" and another for "Ladies and Escorts." There was a restaurant that served Chinese food on Main Street, which was always packed after the dances ended or the bars closed. Blairmore was just far enough from my home in Bellevue that it had a certain exotic aurora to it, like Paris for a farm boy.

HURRY UP AND WAIT: RECRUIT TRAINING IN THE CANADIAN ARMY

It was 1963, getting towards the tail end of the Cold War. My friend Blythe Mattson and I had signed up to take a six-week basic training course in the Canadian Army. The course would be held at CFB Wainwright, east of Edmonton. I had never been farther away from home than Calgary, so I had no idea what to expect at Wainwright—that may as well have been in another country. There was no work for us in the Crowsnest Pass, now that practically all the coal mines had all closed. My dad was trying to sell his business and get ready for a move to Calgary, where I would have to finish high school. It was a time for change.

RCEME cadets in Blairmore; Allan Amos highlighted by arrow
(Photo Credit: Dennis Amos).

"It'll make men of you boys," said Blythe's mom, Huberte Mattson. "Besides, there's nothing for you to do in the Pass, except get into trouble."

In a way, she was right. My dad more or less felt the same way. He had served in the Royal Canadian Navy during World War II, so he had a lot of experience with the military. My mother was worried as usual that this could be dangerous and maybe I could get hurt or something. Mothers always worry about their children, don't they?

The economy in the Crowsnest Pass had hit rock bottom. Many of the large mines had gradually closed, following the shift to diesel locomotives, and there was little work ahead. Granted, the Japanese market wanted good coking coal, of which there was a lot in the Pass, but it would be several years until this market proved out in nearby British Columbia.

Blythe and I would be paid several hundred dollars for taking this training course, which was a veritable fortune in those days. Plus, room and board would be free. This would beat shovelling coal and pitching bales of hay. How could we go wrong?

I had been a cadet in the Royal Canadian Electrical and Mechanical Engineers (RCEME) of the Canadian Armed Forces—Militia in Blairmore in high school, so I had at least some experience with army life and drills, but the thought of the basic training course was too good to believe. Three square meals a day, free. Pay parades every couple of weeks, with a small advance on our salary. A fat cheque at the end of six weeks. More money than I had ever dreamed of before, and a chance to travel and meet some new friends.

Early one Saturday morning, we boarded an army bus in Blairmore. It was a sad moment in a lot of ways when I waved goodbye to my parents. I would be gone for quite a while, and when I returned, there would be some more summer jobs and then it would be off to Calgary and the start of a new life. As the bus headed north, there was a party atmosphere on board. Quite a few of the army recruits from British Columbia were already on the bus, and there were some live wires, to say the least.

At our first rest break at a truck stop near Calgary, I got my first look at how the other half lives. I had always been told to not to steal; the consequences of stealing had always been driven home hard. Like you could go to jail, for starters, plus it was dishonest and wrong. I was surprised at the loot a lot of the BC recruits shoplifted from the service station store. And they didn't try to hide it either. "What, you guys paid for that stuff? Not us!" they bragged. It was to be like that all summer.

The merchants in Wainwright watched us like hawks, and for good reason. You didn't dare leave anything valuable lying around or somebody would steal it. Not that the military wasn't strict. They had stern warnings for anybody caught stealing military property and regularly had surprise inspections where they would look for stolen contraband. If you got caught, it was straight to the brig! The military had its own justice system and were strict disciplinarians. The military police scared the pants off of me.

What a surprise it was to live away from home on a military base. There was no dignity at all in the barracks: the toilets had no doors; open showers; barracks without any private areas, only bunk beds, row after row; and just enough room in the lockers for your military issue clothes and gear, with hardly any room left over for civilian ware. Spartan would be a gracious way to describe the living quarters. It was quite a shock to my system, to say the least. In my mind, the military intended to make it crystal clear that a person belonged to them, heart and soul. "You're in the army now," started to take on a whole new sinister meaning and made a lot more sense in my young mind—nobody pampered you.

The day started early. Revile was at six a.m. A drill sergeant walked through the barracks at about five after six a.m. and woe betides any late risers—it was toilet cleanup detail for them. Breakfast was at seven a.m. Parade square was at eight a.m. and training lasted all morning.

Lunch went from noon to one p.m. More training, drills, and courses went from one p.m. to five p.m. Dinner was at six p.m. Every day, except Saturday and Sunday, the routine was the same. You rushed from one event to the other. "Hurry up and wait" became the order of the day, every day. On weekends, breakfast was an hour later.

I quickly learned how to wash and iron my clothes. If the crease in your pant legs wasn't sharp or your collar wasn't starched just right, you were in trouble, big time. It was kitchen patrol for malingers, or worse—sweeping and mopping the barracks floors. Your shoes had to be polished so the corporal could see his reflection. Your brass had to shine—any tarnish and you would be doing twenty-five push-ups on the parade square. Your putties had to be lined up just right. I always wondered why Canadian soldiers maintained the tradition of the British Army puttees, which were wrapped tightly around the bottom of your pants along the top of your boots. The blankets on your bed had to be just so, or the bed had to be made up again. With my various and assorted altercations with school teachers over the years, I learned fast that the military meant business. Consequently, I went out of my way to be well behaved. You didn't dare laugh or crack a smile when one of your buddies made a mistake. If you got caught smirking, you would be in just as much trouble; anyhow, it could be you next.

The cafeteria food was barely passable some days, and all the food seemed to taste the same, so you really started to appreciate your mother's home cooking. I could see why there were canteens on the base. I wondered if people could actually do this for a living, day after day. The thought of mom's food made me drool! I thought that the summer would never end, at times. What would happen to us if a war broke out? Would we be quickly conscripted into the regular army? Everybody dreaded the thought of a nuclear war with Russia, and nearby Edmonton was known to be a prime target with its large oil and gas refineries.

We pulled into camp at CFB Wainwright in the dark, and we left in the dark with an overnight stay at Currie Barracks in Calgary on the way home. I never did get my bearings the whole time I was at CFB Wainwright. I was used to seeing mountains in the morning, with the sun low on the horizon. Up there on the prairies in east central Alberta, the sun was always high on the horizon and there were no landmarks to help get your bearings. Thank goodness for the compass or I would have been forever mixed up.

Each day was more or less the same as the last: marching drills, parades, first aid classes, and firearms training; what to do in the event of a gas attack or nuclear war; digging slit trenches (i.e., fox holes) and filling them up again; putting on camouflage paint; and more marching. I got to think that the only thing that soldiers did for a living was marching. The "slow march" was the worst. Half the guys just couldn't get it right. A "slow march" was for special occasions, such as when dignitaries paid visits, or for funerals or the like, when your feet are supposed to glide in slow motion before they hit the ground. We learned to march to music. I liked this the best, and it was a lot of fun. "Put your left foot down when the 'drum' goes boom," bellowed the training corporals and sergeants. How many times did they repeat the saying? "If you miss a step, take a half step to get back in step," was a close second. Woe betides the soldier who dropped his rifle. It was quick march around the parade square with the rifle held high. We feared being thrown in the brig and never seeing home again; the constant threats were scary for innocent kids, most of whom were not very street wise, to say the least. The corporals and sergeants were masters at mind games with the young men. They could berate you in so many ways. Every day. Not all of them mind you, but the majority of them were as tough as nails.

Training could be pretty boring, except for the rifle ranges. I liked range work the best. I was a marksman by all military standards, and so was Blythe. Our gopher shooting and grouse hunting had paid off; we were among the top riflemen in the whole battalion. Those were the best days at the army base: shooting at targets on the 100 to 1000-yard ranges, and the pop-up target ranges. Firing automatic Bren guns and the NATO FN. 7 mm semi-automatic rifles.

The summer finally ended, though. We were bused back to Pass on a Saturday morning. We stopped short of the Canadian Army Militia Headquarters in Blairmore. We got out of the bus, formed up like real soldiers, and marched a few blocks to the militia headquarters. I must admit that I felt a lot of pride. I felt much more grown up than when I had left, having gained more self-confidence. In a few short weeks, I was off to live in Calgary and enter another chapter in my life.

I had spent all my childhood and teenage years in the Pass—and what an adventure life had been. That New Year's Day spent unloading a coal truck was to be a life-long lesson that you don't stop working just because you're tired.

LAST SUMMER IN THE PASS—1964

As luck would have it, I was to spend one more summer in the Pass before leaving for good. It turned out that the Alberta Forest Service (AFS) needed some help on a forest fire suppression crew out of Blairmore. I had applied for a summer job with the forestry department before starting university in the autumn. This one was the best one that had come along. It didn't matter that I was living in Calgary at the time. Work was work; you took it where you found it.

The forestry department would provide room and board, and any wages would go directly into my savings account. The fire suppression crew would stay in an industrial trailer at various locations in the Crowsnest Forest Reserve, which straddled the Crowsnest Pass. We would purchase our own food by using a government direct purchase order from local grocery stores. Groceries didn't cost us anything, and we ate like kings. There was no shortage of steaks, chops, chicken, milk, fruit, and fresh vegetables. There would be no cook, however, and we would rotate cooking duties among the crew, in theory. As it turned out, the other crew members weren't much for cooks. I ended up doing most of the cooking, not that I was a great chef either. I would stick to the basics, and with appetites off the Richter scale, resulting from hard work and lots of fresh air, fine cuisine wasn't really an issue.

The job was more or less slave labour, not that the forestry department didn't mean well. They just thought that you would work forever, and then some. There were no regular hours. I think I had one weekend off the whole summer. I worked all day and was on standby after work during the weekdays and each weekend, without pay. There was no such thing as overtime or stand-by pay. So long as the fire hazard was high, the fire suppression crew was on the job—day and night. This was before public service unions had any teeth. There were no trips to town to chase girls or go to shows; you were simply on standby if you weren't working.

The forest rangers were a great bunch to work for. People like Dick Girardi and Fred Facco were legends in their own right and were real professionals. Girardi was stationed in Coleman and Facco at the Castle River ranger station. I admired them, and they never let me down. They did, however, treat the suppression crew like they were their personal slaves at times. If it meant putting in a new cattle guard along the Forestry Trunk Road or picking up stumps and broken limbs along a right of way, it was all in a day's work. Or we might get the nod to paint forestry buildings or rebuild washed-out bridges. We were even tasked with helping a forestry carpenter build a new house at the Castle River ranger station or outhouses for campsites. I think we built something like two dozen outhouses during the summer.

Fortunately, we only had one fire all summer because there was no fire suppression training for me or the crew, which turned out to consist of a crew leader and two helpers. I think that the crew leader had some experience, but it must have been limited. If a fire broke out, we were supposed to work under the supervision of the local forest ranger. We always were at his beckon call, and our trailer was always stationed near a ranger station, which varied depending on the fire hazard and his work load. Whatever I knew about firefighting I had picked up from my dad, who was the chief of the Bellevue Volunteer Fire Department. This came to a head one hot Sunday afternoon, when we were called to our first fire, north of Coleman beside McGillivray Creek. The Coleman Lions Club was having its annual picnic when one of the camp fires got out of hand, starting a small forest fire.

It was too bad that the fire started because Girardi, the local ranger, was going to take us fishing to Window Mountain Lake just before the alarm came in. Off we went. In short order, we arrived at the scene of the fire. About an acre of pine was already ablaze. There was no time spare to contain the fire before it really got out of hand. Fortunately, McGillivray Creek was nearby, so we had a good source of water. Neither the crew chief, nor my helper, knew how to start the water pump. That was where I came in, and in a few minutes, the pump was going and water was going through the hose. The crew chief, Ron Fontana from Coleman, manned the nozzle. Dick asked me and the other crew member, a young fellow from Fernie whose first name was Gordon, to get the "pulaskis" and help put out some spot fires. Gordon and I looked at each other. "What the hell is a 'pulaski,' Gordon?" I said. Never one to be fazed, Dick showed us what they were and how to use them. "Get the Wajax cans too," shouted Dick. I knew that these were portable water pumps, which were shouldered and packed to the fire line. They had a rather short hose, with a hand pump to spray water on hotspots.

Dick had us settled down after a short while, and before we knew it, the fire was under control and quickly put out. We were heroes for the moment, having saved the day at the Lions' picnic. The people couldn't have been more grateful. There were hot dogs and beer for the tired suppression crew. Of course, we had to stay all afternoon to make sure that the fire didn't flare up again. There were some other false alarms that summer, which we would race to at break-neck speeds, only to find out that the fires were out or hadn't even been fires.

When Gordon quit, I managed to get my friend Blythe Mattson hired on as his replacement. I was among my own kind again, and Blythe was a good companion. One day, we were making cement for the walls of a basement for a new ranger station we were building in the Castle River area. This was hardly what you would call fire suppression duties. It was the autumn now. Since the fire hazard had gone down, we had moved camp. It had been snowing all morning, and we were soaked to the skin. We would mix sand and cement in a portable mixing machine and then dump it in a wheel barrow.

We would then haul the wheel barrow to a wall, which we were making out of cinder blocks, and shovel the cement into the holes in the blocks. It was slow, back-breaking work, and we were wet and cold. "It just goes to show you what a guy will do for a buck," said Blythe. He was right. It made no matter that the house was to be moved a few years later to centralize all the rangers in the Bow Crow Forest Reserve in Blairmore. Naturally, this brought back memories of shovelling coal on New Year's Day when I was sixteen.

The forestry department treated me well, and when the job was done, they had a bus ticket back to Calgary waiting for me. Back in the day, the AFS was a first-class outfit and the job on the fire suppression crew was to lead to other jobs, with what was then called the Department of Lands and Forests, and eventually my childhood dream of working as a government biologist. You earned your stripes, but afterwards, you were rewarded when you worked for the AFS, a once proud agency if there ever was one.

6

REFLECTIONS–LIFE AFTER THE PASS

On November 29, 1998, while still a journalist, Senator Paula Simons wrote a column in the *Edmonton Journal* with the headline, "A Golden Age That Never Was," with a byline "Times are tough but it was brutal 50 years ago." The column was about a teenage boy from a dysfunctional nineties family in a Hollywood hit called *Pleasantville*, who becomes obsessed with a *Father Knows Best*-style TV show. Simons wrote that the idyllic lifestyle the boy experienced was largely delusional and an extraordinary number of Canadians were also blinded by the same fantasy that they were under more financial and emotional stress than families back in the 1950s. She maintained that the response betrayed a profound ignorance of North American social history and "a soppy nostalgia for a Golden Age that never was."

While American TV sitcoms of day made out that family life was almost always pleasant and harmonious, such was not the case in the Pass after World War II. I believe that until 1968, the only grounds for divorce were adultery, which meant excommunication for Catholics. Locals absolutely dreaded cancer, heart diseases, and polio for which there were no cures; they were a virtual death warrant. People didn't live in paper shacks, but very few families enjoyed an idyllic or prosperous lifestyle. That's what I've tried to describe in this book—to illustrate the hard times most families experienced. Regardless, most of the kids I grew up with honestly believed that these were some of the best days of their lives and the best of times to grow up in Canada despite the hardships. As Simons wrote, the real Canadian world has never been Pleasantville: "Let's begin, not by romanticizing our past, but by honestly celebrating the tough work our parents and grandparents did to get us here."

What was it about the Pass that attracted folks to settle in the area? Why did people come from all over the world to work in its deadly coal mines? How did the residents handle all of the natural disasters over the past century? While these are rhetorical questions, I don't recall my grandparents ever talking about why they came to the Pass, but I do recall them saying they had no desire to return to the old country. They also feared working in the mines, where their lives hinged on the stupidest miner in the coal shafts. The women, in particular, dreaded the thought of their husbands being killed in mine accidents because there was no real safety net for survivors at the time.

Many successful people were to come from the Pass, which spawned a lot of basically good people and good citizens, some of whom left while others stayed. Some have held important positions in government, industry, and academia. What is about the Pass that brought forth many leaders and just basically good, decent people in Alberta's society—doctors, lawyers, judges, high-ranking government officials and politicians, artists, successful businessmen, fine craftsmen, musicians, university professors, entrepreneurs, teachers and scholars, foresters and biologists? I believe that much of their success was spawned by high standards set by their hard-working parents and grandparents. Many parents indoctrinated their children to get an education so they didn't have to work in a coal mine and would have opportunities for less dangerous jobs.

To use a cliché, I came from the school of hard knocks, where folks learned to appreciate and value what they had. In its own way, the Pass was a bit like Scotland or Cape Breton Island—all fine places to live with great scenery but hard places to earn a living. The coal mines always cycled between boom and bust. The Pass built people's character. It made men out of boys and made tough women stronger. It was "survival of the fittest," as my dad was fond of saying. You had to get tough and harden up. The Pass was no place for sissies and a proving ground for jobs and careers. You learned early in life that life wasn't fair. You didn't stop working just because you were tired. What didn't kill you made you stronger. You developed a philosophy that you had to make the best of a bad situation. My mother would be the first person to remind me to always try to look for a silver lining in every cloud.

After most of the coal mines in the area were shuttered, my father's Bellevue Transfer Company, a small trucking business, went broke. He sold the company and our family home both for a pittance. Who needed coal-hauling trucks? My mother told me that no real estate agent was involved with the sale of the house; it was a cash deal. In 1963, our family moved to Calgary to seek our fortunes. I finished high school at William Aberhart High School. I subsequently went to the University of Calgary, graduating with a bachelor of science degree in zoology, before attending the University of Manitoba for a pre-master of science degree. Afterwards, I returned to the University of Calgary, where I completed a master of science degree in biology. As things turned out, I was the first ever Faculty of Graduate Studies student to receive such a degree from the University of Calgary in 1970.

I consider myself very fortunate to have been able to attend university, which was a privilege in the 1950s. Attending university was not a right, and people did not spout platitudes that you should follow your dreams. I still return to the Pass from time to time to visit old friends and rekindle many fond memories of my youth, but the Pass is not the place it used to be when I grew up there.

In a May 1, 1981, letter to my mother, Florence Kerr, a local historian who was a driving force behind the *Crowsnest and Its People* historical society book, spoke highly of the Department of Culture for funding the Frank Slide Interpretive Centre that tells the story of the Frank Slide and the dramatic history of the Crowsnest Pass. There used to be a black-and-white interpretive photo of my grandfather Albert Radford with some other coal miners at the Bellevue Mine in the lobby of this popular tourist attraction. The Government of Alberta also established the Leitch Collieries Provincial Historic Site on the Police Flats, near Passburg, featuring an early coal mine beside Highway 3—another tribute to pioneers who settled in the Pass.

Life after World War II in the Pass wasn't blissful by any means, but people made the best of tough times and soldiered on, and they coped and stood together despite many hardships. They were yesterday's survivors. Residents of the Pass, past and present, should be rightly proud of their many achievements and legacy.

ACKNOWLEDGEMENTS

Thanks are due to my second cousin Ann Sapeta for providing records related to family relatives in Poland. Another second cousin, Coleen Carlson, provided me with a wealth of information, photographs, and history about the Radford family for which I'm much indebted to her. I'd also like to acknowledge Michael Holloway and H. W. (Hill) Radford for generously providing me key genealogy details and UK census records of the Radford family name.

My old friends and schoolmates Dennis Amos and Tony Stoklosa clarified details related to our time spent in elementary, junior high, and high school. Special thanks are due to Allan (Chuck) Amos in this regard, who kept bringing up events that stirred my memory. I'm indebted to Chuck for providing me with the "The Shoot-out at the Bellevue Café" poem and for his help in many other ways. Thanks are due to Lanny Amos, Dennis's son, for scanning many historic photographs that are featured in this book.

My father completed a Department of Defence Production Personal History Form that contained much of the family history in this book. Library and Archives Canada provided information on his military service.

I'd very much like to thank Isabelle (Belle) Kovach (nee Marcolin) of Hillcrest for researching the names of the elementary school teachers in Bellevue and her help in other ways.

I'd like to thank David McIntyre for permission to quote his "Burmis Tree" essay and for providing the Foreword. Thanks are due to Monica Field, for graciously sharing the opening poem, "Burmis Tree," a fitting tribute to the area fondly known as the Pass, which she wrote impromptu at the deathbed of a close friend who requested it.

Special thanks are extended to the old friends who wrote stories about growing up in the Pass, which is what this book is all about: Allan (Chuck) and Dennis Amos, Marilyn Costigan (nee Svoboda), Louise Costigan-Kerns, Peter Costigan, George Dowson, Jim Jepson, Lawrence Kryzanowski, Jim (Sibby) Svoboda, and Tony Stoklosa.

Lorne Fitch, an acclaimed author from Lethbridge, deserves thanks for writing the testimonial.

Finally, I'd like to thank my wife, Adrienne, who was an ongoing source of encouragement and advice over a long period of time as the book took shape. She was an invaluable research aid, especially concerning archival school records. I can't thank her enough for all the time and effort she put into helping craft the storyline.

Because this project was funded in part by the Government of Alberta, I'd like to thank the following people who wrote letters in support of an Alberta Heritage Preservation Partnership Program (HPPP) publication grant application:

Joey Ambrosi, Facility Supervisor, Frank Slide Interpretive Centre
Allan (Chuck), Dennis and Lanny Amos
Dr. Lawrence Kryzanowski, Senior Concordia Research Chair in Finance
Sharon Lutz (nee Svoboda),
Chris Mathews, Executive Director-Crowsnest Museum
David McIntyre
Ron Montgomery
Mayor Blair Painter, Municipality of Crowsnest Pass and Council
Roger Reid, MLA, Livingstone-Macleod

APPENDIX

FATHER'S PARENTS—RADFORD

It's been said that Canada is a country of immigrants, and for those interested in researching their family history, go for it. It's challenging and interesting to research your family's roots, but anybody can do it. My family history is likely quite similar to many residents of the Pass. Luck plays a role in sourcing key historical information, which can be obtained from different sources, such as family records and the Canadian Museum of Immigration at Pier 21 in Halifax, Nova Scotia.

According to online sources, "Radford" is an English surname deriving from one of several places in England named "Radford," chief among these being Radford, Coventry, and Radford, Nottingham. The most closely related surname to Radford is "Radforth," while a common variant is "Redford."

Based on genealogy research provided to me by H. W. (Hill) Radford, who resides in Regina, Saskatchewan, I am probably an ancestor of William and Sarah Radford, and likely related to their son, John, based on UK census records and some genealogical assumptions.

My father's dad, James Radford, was born on December 15, 1876, in England and arrived in Canada in 1903; he was the oldest in a family of five, with four sisters. He was killed in a mining accident on March 2, 1943, at age 66. Regrettably, I have only some sketchy historical records and some family memorabilia of the man and his wife. My grandmother Radford moved to Calgary where she passed away in 1965.

Fred, Beatrice, Beth, Isabel, Doris, James, Jessie, and Sam(uel) Radford.

Thanks to H. W. (Hill) Radford, who lives in Regina, I have a copy of UK census returns dated 1871, 1891, and 1901, which list a "James Radford" from Birmingham, England. I presume this is where my grandfather came from. On a handwritten census ledger dated 1901, the age of James Radford, was recorded as twenty-three, which matches my grandfather's birthdate, and his occupation was listed as a "gas works labourer."

Birmingham is in west central England, to the northwest of London. James Radford began working for the West Canadian Collieries in Bellevue after a mine explosion in 1910 and was an employee until his accidental death in that mine. He died after being crushed between two mine cars. I didn't know any other details related to his untimely death until I came across the following *Blairmore Enterprise* newspaper account of his death. He must have been quite the guy. He apparently worked in coal mines from when he was eight years old. He came from a family of five with four sisters and emigrated from England with my grandmother. He initially worked at a coal mine in Springhill, Nova Scotia, but didn't like the working conditions, so ventured west to mines at Saskatoon, Saskatchewan, and Kipp, Alberta, returning to Springhill each autumn. His family eventually came west on a Harvest Excursion train in 1912 and took up residence in Bellevue. These trains transported workers from eastern Canada to the prairies to help with the fall harvest. They lived in what's called the "Dairy" area of Bellevue, on the north side of the village. They had a musical family. My dad and Aunt Jessie could play the piano by ear and were good singers.

The following is an excerpt from the *Blairmore Enterprise*, March 5, 1943, page 1, via the Peel Library of the University of Alberta website:

WELL KNOWN MINE MAN VICTIM OF ACCIDENT

A sad fatality occurred in the Bellevue mine of the West Canadian Collieries on Tuesday evening of this week, in which James Radford, one of the best and most popularly known of Pass mining men, was the victim.

It appears that Mr. Radford, in the course of duties as pit boss, was coming out of the workings on a trip of cars moved by a compressed-air motor, which it is presumed jumped the track and the pit boss was caught between the first car and the motor, where he was fatally crushed. T. Sterba, the motor driver, was slightly injured.

An inquest was ordered, and was held before Coroner McPherson last evening, with a verdict of accidental death being returned.

Mr. Radford had been an employee of the West Canadian Collieries for slightly over thirty years. He was born in England sixty-six years ago, and came to Nova Scotia some forty years ago, later moving west. During his time in The Pass, he made numerous friends. He was largely instrumental in the formation of what is now the Bellevue and District Horticultural and Industrial Society and for some years was its very faithful and efficient secretary. He also took a leading part in curling activities and First Aid work, and was a charter member of Bellevue Lodge of the I.O.O.F. [International Order of Odd Fellows].

Surviving are his wife, three sons and four daughters. The sons are James, fire boss at Greenhill mine, Blairmore; Samuel with the Navy, Fred [erick] with the Air Force, and daughters, Mrs. T. [Doris] Bradley [who divorced and later married George Steele], of Winnipeg; [Alice] Beatrice at home [who later married Albert Christie], Jessie in Winnipeg and Mrs. Robert [Beth] Shevels in Bellevue.

Funeral will take place on Sunday at 1 p.m., with service held at the United church. The remains will be laid to rest in the Bellevue cemetery.

According to records written by my father, my grandmother was born on July 2, 1880, and her maiden name was "Smythe." This is contrary to an Anglican confirmation card in family memorabilia, where her name was written as Sarah Isabel Smith. She was confirmed at Chaddesden Church by the Anglican Bishop of Derby on February 23, 1891. She had a sister named Lily, who married and moved to Australia, where she died of "respiratory consumption" (i.e., pulmonary tuberculosis) at age twenty-one, on March 17, 1893.

Records on Ancestry.ca show a "Sarah Isabel Radford" born in 1882, which I believe are in error. Other records provided by my second cousin Coleen Carlson indicate that she was born in 1879 in Spondon, Derbyshire, England. In some family memorabilia, there's a handwritten note that she left England with her husband on April 18, 1903, and arrived in Halifax on May 1 before going to Springhill on May 2, 1903. She was buried in Queen's Park Cemetery in Calgary, where my father and mother rest in peace. There is no trace of her in the UK census records from 1881 to 1901 that Michael Holloway located, which lends support to her birth in 1879. I remember her being a rather stern woman who seemed to feel that children should be seen and not heard. During what I recall as rare visits to her home, the grandkids were usually told to stay in the kitchen or go play outside. We were seldom allowed to sit in the living room, and when we did so, we were told to be quiet, possibly because my brother and I could be rather rambunctious at times.

Isabel and James Radford at their home in Bellevue.

MOTHER'S PARENTS—SAPETA

Online sources indicate that the "Sapeta" family name originated in Poland and is apparently a rare surname. It is the most common surname in Poland of all countries surveyed in the world but is not even mentioned in Austria, where Alberta provincial census records indicate my grandparents may have lived before emigrating to Canada.

Victoria and Albert Sapeta outside their home in Coleman.

My mother's father, Albert Sapeta, was born in 1882 and died on February 18, 1969, at the age of eighty-seven in the Crowsnest Pass Hospital, apparently from a bowel obstruction. Like of lot Pass residents, he often said that people who were admitted to a hospital went there to die. Although 1911, Canadian census records indicate he came from Austria, Papa, as he was affectionately called, was born in Rodziechowy, which is located in what is now southern Poland. I've been told that boundaries changed frequently in this part of the old Austro-Hungarian Empire. He immigrated to Canada in 1906, at the age of twenty-four, being one of the first pioneers to settle in Bushtown, situated in southeast Coleman, not far from the Crowsnest River. He married his wife, Victoria Mika, in Poland in 1906, who joined him in 1909 after crossing the Atlantic Ocean and Canada on the Canadian Pacific Railway alone. She was unable to speak any English at the time.

Grandma was born in 1887 also in Rodziechowy; she passed away in 1973 in Calgary. To put these dates in perspective, it wasn't until 1905 that Alberta became a province. I've often marvelled at their courage to immigrate to an unsettled foreign country where they knew no one and didn't speak the English language. A cousin of mine, Kathy Worth, visited Rodziechowy in 2017, where she was shown the birth certificates of both Papa and Grandma in the local church. She was also shown as an affidavit regarding Grandma's parents' legal sanction of her marriage because she was only nineteen at the time. They never returned to Poland, and neither my grandmother or Papa expressed any interest in doing so. As was the custom at the time, they learned to speak English now that they were in Canada and spoke their native language infrequently.

My grandfather was a coal miner from 1906 until 1925, when he bought and operated the Grand Union Billiard and Bowling Hall, which he re-named Albert's Billiard and Bowling and managed until his death. Granny would often tell me she dreaded the sound of the mine siren because other than signalling whether there was work for the miners, it was also sounded when a mine accident had occurred. While he wasn't a large man, Papa didn't suffer fools gladly. I can clearly remember him running riffraff out his pool hall at the first sign of trouble during times when I visited him to shoot a game of billiards. There was never any charge when I played billiards at his establishment. Once, I visited him in the summer when a thunderstorm occurred, accompanied by a downpour with thunder and lightning. I was standing near the front door when a bolt of lightning hit a nearby power pole a few feet away. Sparks flew, and the pole caught on fire. It was split in half. A terrifying explosion created a ground level concussion, which knocked me to the ground in a daze. All this happened right in front of the pool hall in broad daylight, around the noon hour.

Albert Sapeta's home in Coleman; note the pack horses in front of house.

There was a barn at Papa's home in Bushtown, where my grandmother kept a milk cow and he raised Belgian hares. Papa had several saddle horses pastured nearby, which he used during his big game hunting trips both north and south of Coleman—at a time when there were only bush trails to follow. Interestingly, when I checked online, I found he had his own registered livestock brand, along with his brother, Carl, a rancher who farmed north of Cowley, east of the Crowsnest Pass. Farming back in the day was a hardscrabble existence. Carl and his wife, Stephania, worked long and hard to keep their land, especially during the Great Depression. They raised turkeys as a cash supplement on their mixed farm for many years and at least through the 1950s. I don't think many people nowadays appreciate just how difficult life was for people like my grandparents and the Sapeta family who farmed north of Lundbreck. There was no electricity, indoor plumbing was unheard of, water came from a hand pump near the kitchen, there were no paved roads, and motor vehicles were rare.

Walter (L), Bill, and Steve Sapeta, sons of author's relatives Carl and Stephania Sapeta, with their horse Phoenix on the family farm north of Cowley, 1934.

Papa was an ardent and skilled big game hunter, still hunting bighorn sheep at seventy-six years of age; he climbed Barnaby Ridge in the West Castle River Valley in pursuit of a ram that year. I believe he shot his last deer when he was eighty-four on the TransCanada pipeline right of way near Coleman, which my uncle Carl helped him field dress and butcher. He was still hunting well into his eighties, which was his passion in life.

Papa was a kind man who had a heart of gold. He enjoyed a simple life. Every time I visited him at his home in Coleman, he gave me an American silver dollar. It was not unusual for Pass residents to have a stash of silver dollars because they did not trust banks after they defaulted on deposits during the Great Depression. I eventually cashed them in when I was going to university to help cover my costs, and they yielded several hundreds of dollars in the 1960s, a large amount of money at the time when yearly tuition ran about $300. Papa would take me into the pantry and ask me what kind of bottled pop I'd like to have. This was a real treat, no kidding, because most families made their own pop—root beer—and store-bought beverages were a luxury. Being in the billiards business, he had cases of various brands at his home: Cream Soda, Orange Crush, Hires Root Beer, Coke-a-Cola, and Canada Ginger Ale. Canned pop was yet to arrive. Bottled pop was in small containers. Once we had been watered, it was time to visit and listen to Papa's stories. I guess that Papa was my childhood hero.

He was a big game hunter par excellence. His tales of hunts for bighorn rams and grizzly bears were captivating. They were enough to scare the pants off a kid. Not that he was boastful. No, he was a God-fearing Catholic, hard-working man, and seldom without a White Owl cigar in his mouth—or so it seemed. It was an adventure to visit his home. There were grizzly bear rugs throughout the house and in the porch. A stuffed full-mount mountain goat was in the barn. Saddles, halters, and pack frames hung on the wall of sheds in his backyard, the smell of polished leather in the air. Three trophy bighorn sheep ram heads hung in the living room. Deer antlers were piled in the backyard sheds. A few deer heads hung on the walls inside his home. Papa had learned some taxidermy back in the old country, in Poland.

Once he surprised a big boar in a patch of huckleberries in Gravenstafel Creek, near what is now the Castle River Ski Resort, west of Pincher Creek. The grizzly reared up on its hind legs not fifteen feet away. Papa held his ground and shot it in the neck with a lever action .303 British Winchester carbine rifle. It fell almost at his feet, dead. He had the bear hide to prove it. Whenever we showed up with a cold, he would march out a jar of bear grease. He must have taken a lot of black bears in his days also, judging by the stockpile of bear grease he had in his pantry. He would insist that my mother give us a good rubdown with the bear grease until the cold cleared up. "It's good for you boyses. It will make you feel better," was his advice. In those early days a big game hunt meant riding out from his home in Bushtown with a string of pack horses for weeks on end. There were no roads in the wilderness surrounding the Pass in those days. Travel was by foot and horseback. He always told me, "Duane, if you get lost find a stream and follow it downhill. It will always take you home."

Carrie, Carl, and Alice (L–R, standing), Albert, Victoria, and Helen Sapeta (L–R, sitting).

My uncle Carl, who never married, lived with my grandparents and passed away after having a stroke in 1973. Carl looked after the pool hall after Papa passed away. He was a kind and gentle man, an unforgettable uncle who doted on me as a kid. A carpenter by trade, Carl built a couple of saw horses for me and my brother to play on, complete with wooden saddles and stirrups, reigns, and horse heads. We would play on these sawhorses for hours, imaging we were cowboys when we visited our grandparents' home. He'd often walk us to a café on Main Street (now known as Chris's Restaurant) for soda pop and milkshakes during our frequent Sunday visits, when Carl would generally spoil us rotten. The café was an old-fashioned diner with tables and a counter. My favourite spot was always a stool by the counter so I could watch the waitresses do their job, especially making milkshakes and banana splits.

RESOURCES

FURTHER READING

Cousins, William James, *A History of the Crow's Nest Pass*. Historic Trails Society of Alberta, 1981.

Crowsnest Pass Historical Society, *Crowsnest and Its People*. Alberta: Crowsnest Pass Historical Society, 1979.

Nyland, Tracey, *The Mountain That Walks: Book One*. Independently published, 2020.

WEBSITES

Crowsnest Highway—South Western Canada's Information Resource: www.crowsnest-highway.ca/

Discover Crowsnest Heritage: www.crowsnestheritage.ca/history/bellevue/

Graveyards of Industry—Mohawk Tipple: www.ghosttowns.com/canada/alberta/blairmore.html

Heritage Inventory Project—Phase 2 Municipality of Crowsnest Pass Blairmore and Frank, 2014: www.crowsnestpass.com/public/download/documents/13945

Hillcrest Mine disaster: http://hillcrestminedisaster.com/

Historical Walking Tour of Bellevue pamphlet: www.crowsnestheritage.ca/wp-content/uploads/2010/08/Bellevue-Walking-Tour.pdf

Radford family name origin: www.houseofnames.com/radford-family-crest

Sapeta family name history: www.namespedia.com/details/Sapeta

Shooting the Breeze: www.shootinthebreeze.ca/

The Bunny Bonspiel: https://crowsnestcurlingclub.weebly.com/the-bunny-bonspiel.html

GLOSSARY

Adanac: An open pit mine operated by West Canadian Collieries located south of Hillcrest.

AFS: Alberta Forest Service, formerly a division of the Alberta government responsible for land management in the green (unsettled, forest) zone of Alberta.

AMA: Alberta Motor Association, a non-profit membership organization serving Alberta and the Northwest Territories, founded in 1926.

APP: The Alberta Provincial Police was a police force active in Alberta between 1917 and 1932.

Banjo shovel: A large scoop shovel used to shovel coal.

Bellevue: Bellevue was named after a French expression, "Quelle un belle vue," which in English translates into "What a beautiful view."

Bellevue Fire Brigade: A group of volunteer firefighters.

Bellevue Transfer Company: A small trucking business Sam(uel) Radford bought from Johnny Raymaker.

Bituminous coal: Relatively soft black coal containing a tarlike substance called bitumen; of higher quality than lignite (steam) coal but of poorer quality than anthracite (coking).

Bohunk: Racial slur coined for Bohemians from the Czech Republic; this contemptuous name became "bohonk" in the Pass.

Bunny Bonspiel: Long-standing curling bonspiel held at Easter in Blairmore.

Burmis Lumber Company: Sawmills at Lost Creek and Burmis that had a sawdust burner and milled local lumber.

Burmis Tree: Ancient limber pine that marks the start of the Pass on the Alberta side of the border.

Bushtown: Settlement in east Coleman on both sides of the Crowsnest River.

CFB Wainwright: Canadian Forces Base Wainwright, a military training ground in eastern Alberta.

Chinook winds: Warm winds over the Rocky Mountains that blow into Alberta from British Columbia during the winter.

Coking coal: Metallurgical anthracite coal used in the production of steel.

Crowsnest Pass: A geographic area defined by a legendary southern mountain pass that straddles the border between Alberta and British Columbia; the most southerly pass in Alberta used by railways.

Currie Barracks: Former Canadian Army garrison in Calgary.

Dairy: The "Dairy" is the part of Bellevue north of Main Street, which used to be Highway 3 in the 1950s.

DP: Displaced person; European refugees who emigrated to Canada after World War II.

Emilio "Emperor Pic" Picariello: Legendary, notorious Pass rum-runner during prohibition of alcohol from 1918 to 1920.

Frank Slide: Canada's worst natural disaster, a landslide that fell from Turtle Mountain in 1903, where at least ninety people lost their lives; designated a Provincial Heritage Site.

Gate Night: The night before Halloween, when it was not uncommon for teenage kids to vandalize public property in the Pass.

Grassy Mountain: A West Canadian Collieries open pit mine located north of Blairmore.

Harvest excursion: Before the introduction of the combine, Canadian prairie harvests required large numbers of labourers for short periods of time; Harvest excursion trains brought workers west to harvest grain from 1890–1930.

Hillcrest: Named after the Hillcrest Mines, a town located south of Bellevue.

Hoist: In underground coal mining, a hoist (or winder) is used to raise and lower conveyances within the mine shaft.

Hutterite: A German religious sect whose members reside on separate colonies and practise a traditional way of life.

IOOF: International Order of Odd Fellows, a non-political and non-sectarian international fraternal order founded in 1819 by Thomas Wildey in Baltimore, Maryland, US, that promotes personal and social development.

Joe's Café: Bellevue Café operated by Joe Mah and later his son, Jim; notorious for the infamous shoot-out with immigrant Russian train robbers and local police; designated as a provincial heritage resource by Alberta Culture.

Jules J. Fleutot: The first Bellevue Mine manager and founder; a French national.

Lille: Site of West Canadian Collieries Coal Mine near the headwaters of Gold Creek, north of the village of Frank.

Maple Leaf: The south-eastern part of Bellevue, named after the Maple Leaf Coal Company.

Maple Leaf Collieries: In 1909, the Maple Leaf Coal Company commenced operations at the Mohawk bituminous mine in Bellevue and constructed the settlement of Maple Leaf, adjacent to Bellevue.

Masonic Lodge: Private building or "lodge" used by Masons to hold their fraternal meetings and conduct business that traces its origins to British stonemasons.

Night Riders: A gang of teenage boys from Bellevue and Hillcrest who wore hoods like members of the Ku Klux Klan and rode horses, always at night, to raise a little hell and scare folks.

Nicky Nicky Nine Doors: A game where you gather up a bunch of your friends and go knocking on people's doors and run away, which understandably made the occupants angry.

Rabbit gun: Short barrelled .22 calibre rifle.

RCEME: Corps of Royal Canadian Electrical and Mechanical Engineers provides army engineering maintenance support.

Royal Canadian Legion: An organization for Canadian military veterans and servicemen.

RCMP: Royal Canadian Mounted Police, Canada's national police force.

Slavs: Ethnic group consisting of Russians, Poles, Ukrainians, Yugo-Slavs, Czechs, and Slovaks.

Steam coal: Thermal (lignite) coal, also known as steam coal, is used for power and heat generation.

Tipple: An engineering structure used at a mine to load coal into railroad hopper cars.

West Canadian Collieries: A coal company that operated mines at Lille, Blairmore, Bellevue, and Adanac in the Crowsnest Pass; one of the early mining companies in the Pass founded by French nationals.

ABOUT THE AUTHOR

Duane S. Radford is a native of Bellevue, Alberta, and currently resides in Edmonton, Alberta.

He's an award-winning writer and photographer, who started freelance writing and photography in 1995. Duane was bestowed an Alberta Order of the Bighorn Award, Alberta's foremost conservation award, as a member of the Bow Habitat Station Core Committee, in 1998.

He is a past president of the Outdoor Writers of Canada (OWC). He received the OWC highest award, the Pete McGillen Award, in 2017. He's currently a member of the Writers' Guild of Alberta.

Duane is a member of the Alberta Fish & Game Association (AFGA) and represents this organization on the Antelope Creek Ranch Management Committee. He received the Henry Lembicz— Clean Air, Clean Land, Clean Water award from the AFGA in 2016. In 2019, he received both the AFGA Fulton Award, its highest award, as well as the Canadian Wildlife Federation Roderick-Haig Brown Award, the latter for outstanding communications.

He retired as the director of Alberta's fisheries management branch. He worked as a regional director, regional fisheries biologist, and fishery scientist for Alberta's Fish and Wildlife Division. He is certified as a Fisheries Scientist by the American Fisheries Society. He is an honorary member of the Great Plains Fishery Workers Association.

He has authored 1000+ magazine articles and recipes in various magazines and newspapers in Canada and the United States as well as nine books, five of which have received awards: *Fish & Wild Game Recipes* (2006); *Conservation Pride and Passion: The Alberta Fish and Game Association 1908–2008* (2008), which he co-authored with Don Meredith; *The Cowboy Way* (2014); *The Canadian Cowboy Cookbook* (2014), which he co-authored with Jean Paré and Gregory Lepine; and *Fishing Northern Canada for Lake Trout, Grayling and Arctic Char* (2015), which he co-edited with Ross H. Shickler. He co-authored *Rodeo Roundup* with Wendy Pirk (2016) and authored *Canadian Fly Fishing: Hot Spots & Essentials* (2017). His eighth book, *Hunting Alberta*, was published in 2019 and made Edmonton's Capital City Press 2020 list of feature books. His ninth book, *Canadian Outdoor Survival Guide*, was published in 2021.